—7.

WORLD WIDE SERIES

General Editor: James L. Henderson
Senior Lecturer, Institute of Education, London University

WORLD PROBLEMS

SHEILA GORDON

Department of History
Kingsdale Comprehensive School, Dulwich

B. T. BATSFORD LTD London

A

First published 1971

© *Sheila Gordon 1971*

Filmset by Keyspools Ltd, Golborne, Lancashire
Printed in Great Britain by C. Tinling and Co Ltd, London and Prescot
for the publishers B. T. Batsford Ltd, 4 Fitzhardinge Street, London W1
7134 1572 X

ACKNOWLEDGMENT

The author and publisher wish to thank the following for permission to reproduce the illustrations on the pages indicated: Aerofilms & Aero Pictorial Ltd for page 43; Associated Press for pages 59, 65, 68, 70, 71, 77, 89 and 92; Barnaby's Picture Library for pages 17 and 83; Camera Press Ltd for pages 27, 29, 30, 34, 41, 42 and 51; J. Allan Cash for pages 84–86; Greater London Council for page 45; Keystone Press Agency for pages 22 and 61; Mansell Collection for pages 33, 49 and 76; John McCann for page 44; Oxfam for page 19; Radio Times Hulton Picture Library for pages 37, 38, 53 and 60; Shell Photographic Service for pages 23–26 and 39; St. Louis Post Despatch for page 91; United Nations for the title page and pages 11 (top), 28 and 78; UNICEF for page 11 (bottom) and page 12; United Press International for pages 35, 57, 58 and 88; United States Department of Agriculture for page 82; United States Information Service for pages 75 and 80; The Trustees of the Wellcome Library for pages 7–10; World Health Organisation for page 16.

CONTENTS

FOREWORD

Growing up in the second half of the twentieth century means being globally involved and committed. However localised the lives we lead, these are increasingly influenced by forces which cut right across the traditional divisions of nation, class, race and creed. That is why WORLD WIDE has been chosen for the title of this series. Each volume in it, after Sheila Gordon's general introductory one, *World Problems*, deals with one aspect of the contemporary human scene. It is hoped that these illustrated studies will make an educational contribution to the solution of the problems of mankind's emerging world order.

In *World Problems* Sheila Gordon has drawn on her own experience of the classroom situation to produce a splendidly straightforward and lucid text, intelligible to young people of a broad range of ability. Each chapter begins by placing its theme briefly in historical context and ends with a number of practical suggestions for 'Follow-up Work'. A particular merit of this author's treatment of her material is that, although much of it is inevitably grim, she manages to convey her message, loud and clear, that the world outlook is not hopeless, that its problems are within the compass of man's solution if he so desires. This comes out in her chapter on the environmental predicament of humanity, which is so frequently being discussed at the present time.

What distinguishes Sheila Gordon's work from most other efforts to meet this educational need for accurate and digestible material on world affairs is the quality of her writing: apart from being well-informed, it is imbued with a feeling of cultural depth. In her final selection she brings out vividly the inter-dependence of man and his environment:

'Perhaps it would be as well if we learned from primitive man to think again of the earth as our mother, and to treat her not with the casual arrogance of spoiled children, but with the love and respect her generosity deserves.' (p. 74)

As readers get to know the contents of this book, they will learn 'the first of all democratic doctrines, namely that all men are interesting.' (G. K. Chesterton)

James L. Henderson

INTRODUCTION

Over 3,000 million people are alive now on this planet. Every year, fewer people die, more babies survive. They are all unique personalities, with customs, ideas and beliefs varying not only from country to country, but from village to village, street to street. Sometimes the differences interest and attract us; more often they seem to disturb us; make us angry; even lead to violence and war. Because of this, it is essential to understand these differences and, equally important, the things that make us kin —our common need for food, living-space and shelter, our desire to bring up our children in safety, our will to survive.

In the old days people could still be largely self-sufficient, growing their own food and making their own clothes, depending little on people outside their own parish or town.

We can no longer do this. There are too many of us to live without reference to others, and the problems of survival in the modern world are too formidable. Science and technology have given us the promise of a better life; but there are millions still whose lives are stunted by hunger, poverty and disease. Even in countries where the majority enjoy a good standard of living—the 'affluent societies'—there are problems: the stresses of overcrowding, the spoiling of the environment by the poisonous wastes of industry and traffic. And over all of us, everywhere, hangs the threat of destruction; we have learnt all too well how to hurt, to frighten and to kill.

Whoever we are, wherever we live, we cannot be sure of escaping these problems. Alone we are nothing; but together we have a chance to overcome them, and we have the knowledge of scientists, engineers and economists to help us. Moreover, many of us today are better equipped than ever before to work for our survival. Because we no longer need to spend all our working hours working on the land or in the factory, we have time and energy to spare—we can afford a concern and compassion for other people.

This book is an attempt to introduce some of the fundamental problems of the struggle to build a more generous, united and peaceful world, and to show their development, their complexity and their challenge.

This doctor looks to the stars for help with his medical knowledge.

1 DISEASE

Disease is as old as life itself. Every living organism is threatened by it. Man is unique only in the extent to which he has consciously tried to understand and to avoid the diseases that endanger his survival.

His earliest recorded efforts at the art of medicine seem somewhat odd to us now. The ancient Egyptians, trying to find some explanation for the illnesses that befell them, hit on the idea that they were caused by spirits; and that, to even things up, there were certain gods who fought these spirits on man's behalf. The doctors, latching firmly on to this idea, spent a lot of time not in treating their patients, but in talking nicely to the gods, and in trying to please them with suitable charms and amulets. We may scoff, but we should remember that these men were pioneers, and did not have, as we do today, the learning of generations of scientists to enlighten them. We might also remember that their practice of embalming their dead taught them much about human anatomy, and that their surgery was remarkably skilful. They also discovered the value of various drugs we still use today—castor oil and opium, for instance.

A doctor's life, even in those days, was daunting in its responsibilities. When King Hammurabi of Babylon drew up his famous code of laws, he suggested that, for a doctor who operated on a citizen who later died, the amputation of his hands might be a suitable punishment. (If the patient were a mere slave, however, the doctor was simply expected to provide a new one and the matter would be considered closed!)

The ideas of doctors in Europe several hundred years later seem equally odd. They

7

had adopted the ideas of Aristotle (a Greek philosopher) and believed that the world and everything in it was made up from the four elements—earth, air, fire and water. Human beings were included in this system, and good health, they thought, could only be ensured by keeping the four elements in a judicious balance. Disease was caused by imbalance, and called for remedies which were usually very nasty and often useless. 'Cures' were usually due only to the remarkable powers of recovery of the human body!

BEGINNINGS OF MODERN MEDICINE

Aristotle's ideas on medicine did not prove to be all that valuable in the long term, but there was another man living in Greece at more or less the same time, with whose ideas and outlook we feel much more at home. His name was Hippocrates. He was not interested in inventing elaborate theories and making facts fit in with them. He was interested in the facts themselves. He observed his patients carefully, recorded in detail what he saw, and drew conclusions from the evidence. This was the same objective, experimental approach that scientists use today, and Hippocrates is often called 'The Father of Medicine'. It was this approach, revived again by seventeenth-century scientists, that provided the basis for the discoveries that were to lead to a really effective attack on the tyranny of disease.

Vaccination 'en masse' in the East End of London, 1871.

This is the hand of Sara Nelmes. It was from these cowpox pustules that Edward Jenner took the lymph for his first vaccination against smallpox.

The great medical discoveries of the modern world have come from scientists who, like Hippocrates, used their eyes, and kept their minds alert. Think, for instance, of Edward Jenner (1749–1823), a busy country doctor who refused to dismiss as an old wives' tale the belief that a dose of cow pox was a protection against small pox, and instead investigated it. Though he did not fully understand the causes of the immunity, he went on to develop a vaccine which protected people against that often deadly and always disfiguring disease.

The same sort of inspired awareness of the connection between hitherto unrelated facts can be seen in the development of antiseptics.

In the first half of the nineteenth century Ignaz Semmelweiss, a Hungarian doctor who specialised in obstetrics, noticed that one of the two maternity wards in his hospital had three times more cases of puerperal fever than the other. Puerperal fever was a dangerous illness, which often attacked women who had recently had babies, and was caused, as we now know, by germs harboured in bed-linen, surgical instruments, even the midwives' hands. Usually in those days a midwife delivering a baby, like a surgeon amputating a limb, thought that the time to wash their hands was *after* the operation, not before!

The midwives in Semmelweiss's hospital must have been more than usually careful, for in their ward the incidence of puerperal fever was low, but it was high in the ward where the medical students worked. Could it be, Semmelweiss wondered, that there was a connection between the death rate in that ward, and the fact that the medical students came there straight from dissecting dead bodies in the anatomy laboratories? He asked all the students to wash their hands in chloride of lime before going into the ward, and at once the death rate dropped dramatically. He had established the link, though again without understanding exactly what it was that caused the disease.

Louis Pasteur (1825–95) in France was able to provide some of the answers when he observed through his microscope tiny living organisms at work in fermenting wine. He went on to establish that these 'germs', as he called them, caused not only fermentation in wine but putrefaction in a wound.

This discovery fitted in with what the great English surgeon Joseph Lister had deduced from his observations—that there was 'something in the air' which led to the festering of the wounds left by surgery. He was able to put the theory into practice, carefully swabbing out wounds with carbolic acid, and dressing them with carbolic soaked lint, so killing the bacteria and allowing the wound to heal healthily. Although

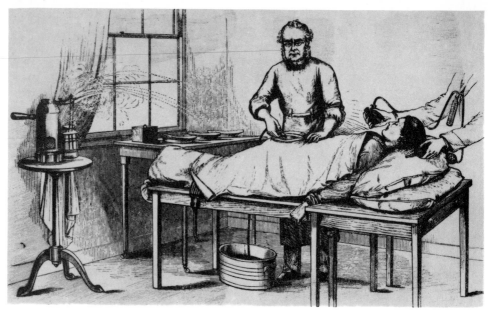

A surgeon operating after the introduction of chloroform and the carbolic spray. This patient had a good chance of recovery.

it took many surgeons a long time to accept it, this was a major advance in medicine, and increased enormously our chances of living to old age. It was a result of the sort of close observation and intelligent deduction that would have delighted Hippocrates.

DISEASES IN THE TROPICS

Everybody living in the richer countries of the world is benefiting directly from these and countless other later discoveries, especially from the discovery of antibiotics which has given us control of many of the 'killer' diseases. We are still apprehensive of serious illness, but at least we know that, if we do become ill, we shall be nursed competently in clean hospitals, be anaesthetised for our operations, and have thousands of drugs available to cure us and relieve our pain. But we have already seen that the world is not a tidy place and that not every country has been able to advance at the same rate as ours. There are still places where, because of poverty and lack of doctors, people cannot benefit from the discoveries of modern medicine, and where the quality of life is impoverished by diseases we have never known.

Look at the picture opposite. We might think on looking at this appalling disfigurement that it must have been caused by a rare disease. Yet this is a woman with yaws, and we know that as late as 1955 about 50 million people in the world were suffering from it. It is caused by a tiny organism entering the bloodstream through a cut or sore. The first symptom seems harmless enough—just a cluster of small pimples—but gradually the pimples become boil-like sores which spread over the whole body, and these become ulcers that eat into the muscles and finally attack and deform the bones.

Treatment came too late for this Haitian woman. Her face is now permanently disfigured from yaws.

These Unicef workers in Haiti examine children for yaws, so that they can catch the disease early and cure it.

Every house in this Iranian village was sprayed with DDT, in the campaign against malaria.

12

Any village blighted by yaws is run down, squalid, and poverty-stricken. People with wasted limbs cannot work in the fields, and people suffering from a disease they accept as incurable have no interest in working for an uncertain future.

Fortunately the treatment of yaws is one of the success stories of modern tropical medicine. It can be cured by a single massive injection of penicillin. Nowadays wherever yaws is still found, so are teams of doctors and nurses, involved in a world-wide campaign to wipe it out. The medical team first of all explains to the headman of a village that they could bring a cure to his people. They persuade him to call his villagers together and convince them that they should come for examination. In two days a whole village can be examined and treated—can be released from the horrible effects of a disease that had threatened them for centuries.

THE FIGHT AGAINST MALARIA

We tend to think of disease threatening individual people—we think of their personal distress. We should remember that a disease can impede the progress of a whole nation.

Malaria, for instance, has always been the curse of the warm wet regions of the world. Twenty years ago it affected 300 million people every year and killed three million of them. Even those who recovered had further attacks throughout their lives, which lowered their resistance to other diseases. Malaria-infested regions are nearly always underdeveloped regions, because, although the people themselves may not realise it, their will to work and to make progress is sapped by their illness.

From the earliest times that Europeans began to travel and settle in these regions, they searched for a cure for the debilitating effects of malaria. All kinds of causes for it were suggested. The most common idea was that it came from an unseen vapour, or 'miasma', and on Lander's voyage up the Niger in 1832 chloride of lime was sprinkled on the decks to soak up the mysterious dew. Oddly enough, although in the 1840s malaria was being treated by European colonists with useless remedies like saline drinks, and shaving off the hair, the Indians in South America had for years been treating it with some success. They had discovered the effectiveness of a medicine derived from the cinchona or fever-bark tree. Although the essential ingredient of this medicine—quinine—had been isolated as early as 1820, it was not until the second half of the century that it was to be found in the medicine chest of every explorer and colonist. They now had some help against their attacks of malaria, but the people who lived all their lives in the countries they visited—who suffered from it in their millions—were too poor to buy it.

It was not until 1890 that the real cause of malaria was discovered by Sir Ronald Ross. He found that it came not from some mysterious miasma, but from a species of mosquito—the anopheles mosquito. This small and insignificant insect bites malaria victims and sucks up malaria microbes from their blood. These microbes develop inside the insect, and are then transferred to the bloodstream of the next person it bites—and so the cycle of infection continues.

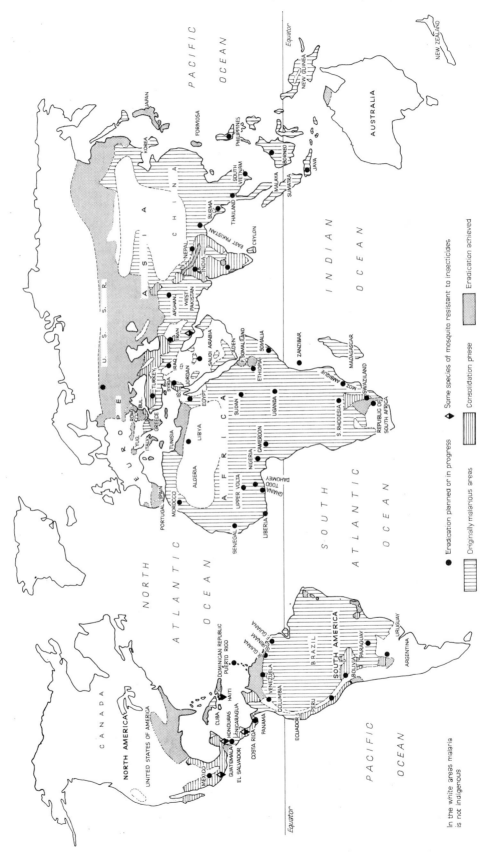

This map shows the extent of the world's malaria problem, and the progress that is being made towards its eradication.

In the white areas malaria is not indigenous

● Eradication planned or in progress

▦ Originally malarious areas

◆ Some species of mosquito resistant to insecticides

▥ Consolidation phase

▨ Eradication achieved

During the Second World War (1939–45) new drugs were discovered which, if taken regularly, could prevent people in mosquito-infested regions from contracting malaria. They, too, cost more than most people living there could afford, so it was decided to attack the disease at its source—to eliminate the anopheles mosquito. The weapon was a powder discovered in the last century but only developed during the war—DDT. DDT is not a medicine but an insecticide. It destroys any insect that comes in contact with it. If a surface is sprayed with DDT all the mosquitoes landing there during the next six months will be killed. It was decided that if whole countries could be treated in this way, they could be freed not only from mosquitoes but from malaria, and a great campaign began.

The campaign needed organising on a world-wide scale. It was mounted by the World Health Organisation (WHO), the agency of the United Nations specially formed to help all countries, particularly the poor ones, fight disease.

Teams of experts were sent all over the world to any country which asked for help. By 1950 anti-malaria teams were at work in India, Afghanistan, Pakistan, Thailand and Sardinia. They went out to remote villages, deep into swamp and jungle, travelling in trucks, boats, helicopters; on mules, camels and elephants. As in the fight against yaws, it was vital to get the cooperation of the people. They, after all, were used to malaria, they accepted it stoically as incurable, but somehow they had to be persuaded out of their apathy. Gradually their cooperation was won and the campaign went on relentlessly. It began to seem that, with enough energy and enough insecticide, man and not the mosquito would win.

But in 1951 entomologists working in Greece noticed something ominous. Some anopholene mosquitoes were becoming immune to DDT, and further investigations confirmed this. It was a terrible blow. Newer types of insecticide were tried, but again some mosquitoes developed a resistance. These immune species, reproducing at a colossal rate, would soon reinfect the areas already cleared—the hardly won successes would be futile.

Then came a gleam of hope. It was discovered that in some areas which had been intensively sprayed with DDT over several years, spraying could be stopped for a whole year without any new outbreak of malaria. So many malaria microbes had been destroyed that the cycle had been broken. The conclusion was obvious. Malaria must be wiped out all over the world before insecticide-resistant mosquitoes became too numerous.

This battle is still going on. In 1955, 250 million people were thought to be suffering from malaria—six years later the figure had dropped to 140 millions. Richer nations were helping the poorer ones to meet the high costs of the campaign. Healthier people meant that more land could be farmed, roads and dams could be built. Countries were at last being freed from the stranglehold of malaria.

Yaws and malaria are only two of the diseases that attack people living in the tropics. There are many others. Cures for some of these diseases are now known and, thanks largely to WHO, are increasingly available, but they can be lastingly effective only if the people themselves are educated sufficiently to understand in what sort of

A hygiene lesson for Nigerian schoolchildren.

conditions the diseases thrive, and help to change them. Medicine may cure a case of round-worms, but only good standards of hygiene will prevent them from returning. A stay in hospital with a regulated diet can cure a baby of kwashiorkor, but only the mother's understanding of the baby's need for protein as well as starch, will ensure that he survives and grows into a healthy adult.

THE DISEASES OF AFFLUENCE

We of the richer nations have been fortunate. We have learned some of these lessons already. It took us many centuries to overcome our own ignorance and superstition, and even now most people have some very odd and unscientific ideas—'old wives' tales'—about health and hygiene.

Moreover we have our own problems born not of poverty but of affluence.

Few doctors today in the United Kingdom see cases of malnutrition. Rickets, the vitamin-deficiency disease so common during times of unemployment and depression before the war, has virtually disappeared. But now many doctors are worried by the increasing number of children and adults who are overweight, and therefore likely to develop heart-disease, and other dangerous conditions, in later life.

16

It is very pleasant to have shops full of sweets, and money to buy them; not so pleasant to have thousands of young people needing false teeth because of dental decay, before they leave school.

We are fortunate that most of us earn enough money for a few luxuries but not so fortunate that one of our most common luxuries—cigarettes—contain tars that can cause cancer. Lung cancer kills—very painfully—25,000 people in the UK every year, and, despite the great campaign to warn people of the dangers, despite the fact that a high percentage of doctors who see the effects of the disease have cut out smoking, there has been no appreciable decrease in cigarette sales.

Life in a modern industrial country is varied, stimulating and for most of us, most of the time, great fun. But for many of us at some time in our lives, it will become too hurried, too complex. We shall have to rely on tranquillisers to calm us, and stimulants to pep us up. Some of us may become part of the half-million people in England and Wales or the million in the United States who need some degree of help from the mental health services.

We may feel compassion for the undernourished child in Brazil and the leper in Nigeria, but we have no reason to feel superior!

However advanced medical science becomes, however long our lives are prolonged, there are many problems still to solve, many of them resulting from the advances themselves.

We have seen how mosquitoes developed a resistance to malaria. In the same way viruses and bacteria can develop immunity to drugs like penicillin. New formulations of drugs are constantly needed to beat these persistent viruses. Doctors are beginning to let comparatively mild illnesses like tonsillitis take a natural course rather than attack them with a powerful drug which may, with over-use, give the patient less protection in subsequent illnesses.

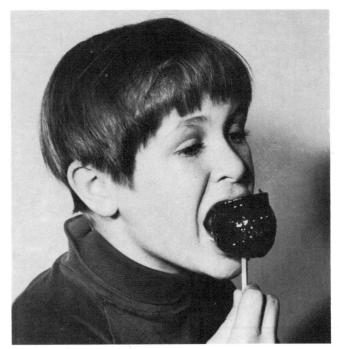

This boy is lucky to have money to spend on a delicious toffee apple—unlucky in that he will probably need false teeth before he is middle aged.

There are still great question marks overshadowing our many success stories.

Despite sophisticated surgical techniques, new drugs, and screening for early diagnosis, cancer still kills 100,000 people a year in Britain alone.

Machines for renal dialysis can purify the blood and save the lives of people suffering from certain kidney diseases, but they are very expensive, and there are not enough for all the people who need the treatment.

The great new surgical success of the sixties—transplant surgery—by which diseased organs of the body, like hearts and kidneys, can be replaced, is also very expensive. Many people are questioning whether the limited amount of money available for research should not rather be spent on less spectacular projects which will benefit more people.

Disease is a cunning enemy—always changing, unexpected, always presenting us with new problems. It causes perhaps less unhappiness and degradation in the world than it did, but it is by no means conquered. The age-old battle goes on.

FOLLOW-UP TOPICS

Find out more about the discoveries of Harvey, Jenner, Lister, Pasteur, Robert Simpson, Alexander Fleming.

Make a study of the work of WHO in one underdeveloped country.

What facilities are provided in your area for chest X-rays, cervical smears, general health check-ups.

Do you know any 'old wives' tales' about health? Do you think they are true?

Make a collection of newspaper cuttings on transplant surgery. Do you think it is worthwhile?

Arthur Swinson, *The History of Public Health* (Wheaton).
James Hemming, *Mankind against the Killers* (Longmans).
Désirée Eduardo-Rees, *The Story of Nursing* (Constable).
David Le Rai, *Modern Medicine* (Wheaton).
F. George Kay, *The Conquerors of Disease* (Max Parrish).
Tony Osman, *In Aid of Surgery* (Phoenix).
Nesta Pain, *Louis Pasteur* (A. and C. Black).

This little Venezuelan girl is suffering from malnutrition. Although she is two years old she weighs only 10 lbs.

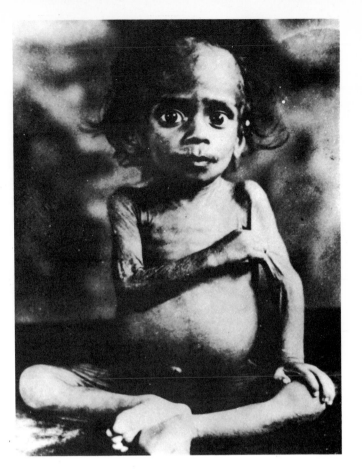

2 HUNGER

It is hardly surprising that we in Britain, the United States, or any of the so-called 'developed' countries, have over the centuries managed to organise a comfortable, secure, and varied pattern of living. We have been fortunate in our surroundings. Our climates are relatively easy; we have good supplies of water, timber, and minerals, and soils in which farmers can sow seed with a fair chance of reaping a good harvest.

But think for a moment of people who have not been so lucky—a Peruvian worker, for instance, queuing for a job, while his wife queues for water at a communal tap that runs for only three hours a day; a Kenyan farmer who sees his tall stands of maize torn to shreds by a swarm of locusts; an Indian couple who know that the failure of the monsoon will mean their children wailing with hunger.

Most of us at some time or another have turned our eyes away from the starving children who stare out at us from posters and newspapers. They remind us too sharply for comfort that our part of the world is sheltered and privileged compared with theirs, and it is tempting to try and convince ourselves that they are not really our problem. Yet can we really live with an untroubled conscience in a world where half the people go to bed hungry, where children die of starvation every day? Can we expect to live in peace while this great gap between the 'haves' and 'have-nots' breeds jealousy, resentment, and unrest?

19

It is *not* just their problem, it is ours too—a world problem, and we need to understand it. Only by first understanding why people go hungry can anything be done —can enough food be grown in every country to feed their fast-increasing populations.

THE INHERITANCE OF THE PAST

Three-quarters of the world's people live in family-units on small plots of land, which they work to provide food for themselves. Any small surplus they can spare they sell in the local market, so that they can afford the few necessities for their extremely simple existence. This is what is meant by 'subsistence agriculture'. It is a way of life that differs little from that of the earliest farming communities thousands of years ago. Because the land is often poor, and their plots so small, they can only produce enough food for themselves; they cannot even grow enough to spare for fodder to feed livestock so they have very little meat or milk. The farmer and his family work hard, just to stay alive.

For centuries this system of farming worked well enough. Indeed in many ways, these farmers, with their primitive tools and simple methods, gained knowledge from which we all benefit—anyone who hoes a row of potatoes to encourage the roots to grow is using a technique developed by Inca farmers working in the Andes over a thousand years ago—but this traditional way of farming simply cannot meet the needs of our world today.

Until very recently the number of people in the world increased only slowly, but now we face a population explosion. In 1900 there were roughly 1,600 million people —today there are 3,200 million, and by the year 2000 the number will have doubled again. Unfortunately the countries whose populations are increasing most rapidly are the very countries where farmers cling most fiercely to the old ways. The land farmed according to these traditional subsistence methods cannot give them all a living, and the drift to the cities has already begun. Once there, people can no longer grow food for themselves: they depend on what the remaining farmers can provide. It is no longer enough to feed one family from one plot of land; it must somehow be made to feed five or even ten families.

The subsistence farmer steers a knife-edge course between survival and disaster.

The failure of the rains can mean the ruin of his staple crop. Farmlands throughout the Middle East, half of Africa, and three-quarters of Pakistan and India are periodically threatened by the desert locust, that destroys months of laborious cultivation in a matter of hours.

Political unrest, riots, and wars like those in Nigeria and Vietnam mean that food supplies are disrupted, or stretched beyond survival point by the influx of refugees.

These are only a few of the things that can happen, and, when they do, people go hungry.

Even when stomachs are full, they are not necessarily full of the right food. Many diets are not only monotonous compared with ours, but often lacking in the protein and vitamins essential to growing children and healthy adults. Sometimes there is no adequate supply of milk to replace the mother's when a baby is weaned. Sometimes mothers feel that meat and fish are bad for their babies. Infants in Thailand for example are traditionally fed on a diet of rice-water, hot peppers, and bananas. The death rate in these countries is high, often as much as 50 per cent for children under five. The diseases that kill them are often the diseases of malnutrition, like kwashiorkor, which causes anaemia and enlargement of the liver.

Moreover, the future of those who survive is uncertain. Modern research suggests that mental development is damaged by malnutrition as well as physical growth, and resistance to other diseases, like malaria, is seriously weakened.

HOW THE FARMER SEES IT

The need for radical change may seem obvious enough to us, but to the farmer working in Africa or South America, or any of the places where farming is bound by ancient traditions, change is often something to be resisted and feared rather than welcomed. Certainly he knows his land is poor, knows it from bitter back-breaking experience. Perhaps it lacks the minerals essential to the growing crop, perhaps there's not enough rain—or too much, so that the good soil is washed away. To a scientific expert in agriculture—an agronomist—the remedies are known, and often quite simple:

    chemical fertilisers to improve the crops and increase their yield;

    irrigation schemes to provide water in controlled amounts;

    new strains of seed to suit a particular soil and climate;

    pesticides to ensure that the harvest goes to feed people and not insects.

And yet, how to get the farmer to adopt these improvements, how to convince him that they *are* improvements, and that he can afford them?

There are not enough trained agronomists to do the persuading, and even where there are, how can the farmer be expected to pay for these things? Why should he risk borrowing from his local money-lender at high rates of interest just to grow more food for people he has never seen?

If he does produce a good crop with a surplus to sell, he cannot sell it directly to the towns and cities, where it is most needed; roads are poor and he has no transport. If he sells in the local market in the normal way, won't there be a risk of a glut and falling prices? And finally, how much of the profit will be his, and how much will have to go to pay off the local money-lender? If we think about it we can see their point; we can see too what a slow and complicated task it is going to be to modernise agriculture successfully on hundreds of thousands of farms throughout the world.

Even where the organisation of men and materials exists to tackle the job, where change ought to be coming quickly, there are other objections and anxieties stemming from religious beliefs.

To the orthodox Hindu, for instance, the cow is a sacred animal. There are over 200 million cattle in India, allowed to wander free, eating more food than the people.

Hindus would be reluctant to drive this sacred bull off the street.

They produce no milk, they spread disease, and they hold up the traffic, yet very few Hindus would dream of killing one even to save it from slow starvation—even if they were themselves starving—because its life is sacred.

In Thailand, anti-malaria campaigns drew serious objections from the many devout Buddhists who believe that the taking of any form of life is wrong—even the life of the malaria-carrying mosquito.

To us these attitudes may seem odd, and many people unfortunately are tempted to scoff and feel superior, to go ahead and force people into schemes that offend their deeply held beliefs. We must remember that our own ideas often seem equally strange to them, and that these faiths that we may sometimes ridicule, sustain them, and give them the courage to face difficulties and disasters that we have never experienced.

In all the underdeveloped countries attitudes to many things will have to change, but they will have to be understood and respected too. Inevitably it is going to take time, and time is all too short. It is a job that calls for great skill and imagination, as well as enormous resources.

ONE EXAMPLE OF SUCCESS

Lying in the hills of Tuscany in northern Italy is a village called Borgo a Mozzano. Fifteen years ago a great many of the characteristics of subsistence agriculture could

22

be seen in this remote place. The land had been farmed for centuries in the same way, small plots being worked as a family concern to produce the family's food. This way of life was simple, but adequate and safe—safe until the population started to increase faster than the food supply.

In 1954 an oil company with interests in agriculture decided to adopt Borgo for a study of the problem, which was common to many parts of Italy, and to observe in this one small community how new techniques and ideas would affect the lives of its people. Their approach was unusual; they did not want to invade the village, telling everyone what to do, but to win the farmers' interest, to get them to cooperate of their own free will, and to introduce the changes themselves.

In May, an agronomist arrived, and settled without fuss into Borgo. He spent his time moving about, studying the soil, the water supply, the way the farmers worked.

These peasants owned their own land, but their small plots were often divided: a man might have a bit of land in three or four different places, and have to move with his tools from one part of the district to another, and Tuscany is mountainous country. Most farmers owned olive trees, and the oil they produced was of a particularly good quality, but it did not occur to them to sell it in markets where good oil was scarce, and so make a profit; instead they produced just enough for themselves.

Borgo a Mozzano—the village that raised its living standards by adopting new farming methods.

They also grew cereal crops, again mostly for their own consumption. The yield was low because, as the agronomist discovered, the seed they used was poor, and hardly any fertiliser was used to make the crops grow well.

They used very few machines. The village was down at heel, and its inhabitants had little interest in new ideas, in education and in craftsmanship. This was what the agronomist had come to study, and what he hoped to see changed. If only a new spirit could be encouraged in the people they could change from peasant farmers into modern productive farm managers.

He gave nothing away—no free gifts of seed or fertiliser. He ventured an opinion when it was asked for, but spent most of his time working his own plot of land, waiting over the months for the questions to start.

Gradually he became accepted, and people began to pass the time of day with him, interested in what he was doing there.

The first sign of change came when ten farmers decided to take up the agronomist's suggestion of trying a new type of maize seed. There was no general rush to act on his suggestion, but at least it was a start. And of course when their crop grew and ripened to give a harvest double the previous weight, the villagers began to think there might be something in these new-fangled ideas after all. Soon the local method of wine-making was brought under scientific control. A better standard was achieved and the wine could now be sold outside the village. Old olive trees were replaced, pesticides used to protect them, and the yield of olive oil was tripled. A

Better varieties of seed have brought this farmer a greatly increased maize crop.

Villagers in Borgo worked without pay to build a new road to replace the old mule track.

new source of wealth was found in the growing of medicinal herbs, which could be sold to the pharmaceutical industry.

At first these changes came from the initiative of a few individual farmers, but once they and their neighbours realised how they could prosper, they began to work together, to cooperate. They devised a plan to irrigate the land in the dry summers; three hundred of them sweated to turn a mule-track into a proper road to link the village with the main road down in the valley; and they clubbed together to buy machinery—a truck, a tractor, and motor-winches to help with difficult hillside ploughing. With their cattle better fed and the size of their herds increased, they realised they could make a profit from selling milk, so they formed a cooperative, with sufficient capital to build good sheds, provide milking machines, and a regular milk-run to market. A domestic science teacher was invited to the village, to advise the womenfolk how to manage poultry and how to improve their families' diet.

All this happened in a remarkably short time. In 1955 the income of the village had been 825,000 lira, but by 1959 it had reached 93,491,400 lira—a hundredfold increase! A remote village with its roots in the middle ages had been transformed by the guidance of one agronomist and by the work and will of the farmers themselves, into a thriving community with a new interest in itself, in farming, in education; able to hold its own in the modern world. Now it is their turn to show others the

An agronomist shows a farmer's wife in Borgo how to test the fat content of her milk.

way; Borgo a Mozzano has become a centre of study for visitors from all over the world, and an example that others are already learning to follow.

This story of Borgo highlights many of the problems involved in gearing simple farming communities to the demands of a hungry modern world. Let us now have a look at these problems on a much larger scale—that of the vast, age-old civilisation of India, as she struggles to feed her people. What are her difficulties and how are they being overcome?

FOOD SUPPLIES IN INDIA

India is a vast country—over a million square miles, but only half of that area is cultivated, and it has to feed over 500 million people. Even when new land is reclaimed the problem remains, for India's population is increasing by 13 million a year. It is not surprising that the average income per head today is only 481.5 rupees (£22) a year.

Population is the key problem for modern India, as it is for so many underdeveloped countries struggling to organise better lives for their people.

To many an Indian peasant, sweating on his small plot of land for pitifully small harvests, the future is certain only in its harshness, and in its unpredictable disasters. A large family not only brings warmth and interest to his life, it provides more pairs of hands to help him, and gives him some kind of insurance and hope for his old age. This is a belief as old as India itself, and we meet it in any community where life is hard and uncertain. What is *new* is that, because of modern medical knowledge, fewer of his children are dying in infancy, and he himself can expect to live longer. This means that the balance between the supplies of food that India can produce and what her people need has been upset—disastrously.

Many Indian rural families, just like English ones during the eighteenth century, flock to the great towns, like Calcutta and Bombay, hoping that the new factories and projects of India's Industrial Revolution will give them the chance of a better life. Jobs are hard to find, and those who do find employment find that food in the town is in short supply and therefore dear. The result is overcrowding and poverty. In Calcutta, for instance, a million people sleep on the streets every night, getting work only occasionally, and reduced to begging for their food. Grain is in such short supply it has to be rationed—one kilogram of wheat and one of rice per person per week.

India is a land where suffering and hardship have always been the lot of the vast

If you lived in India, your water supply would come from a public pump. In times of drought you would have to queue for it.

Drilling for water in Madras, India—a project assisted by the United Nations development programme.

majority, and acceptance of that suffering has been the foundation of the Hindu religion. Yet now in the twentieth century many Indians are no longer content to accept poverty and hunger as their inevitable fate, and India is becoming a country of urgency and change.

In a way the changes started in the days of British rule. British officials were content to keep Indian industry at only a primitive level—it meant more markets for British manufactured goods—but they were nevertheless prepared to help with the development of Indian agriculture. British engineers transformed the Indus valley by vast irrigation schemes that were themselves inspired by Indian irrigation works of medieval times. From 1889–98 they transformed a semi-desert into a land that could support ten times its previous number of people. But it was only a beginning. Today the need for productive land is even more urgent, and the government of a now independent India is tackling the problem on a gigantic scale, not only with big spectacular schemes, but by sinking thousands of wells so that the peasants are no longer dependent on the capricious monsoon to bring water to their crops.

Water is essential for good crops, but of little use if the soil is exhausted and infertile. If India is to achieve its aim of doubling grain production, and so avoid the tragic death-rolls of the 1964 and 1967 famines, many more millions of acres of barren soil must be brought back to life.

To do this the government is investing money in building fertiliser plants, and in importing vast quantities of fertiliser from abroad.

Yet this too is only a start. The government has also to persuade the farmer that

28

fertilisers really do work, and help him to afford them by lending him money. For whatever splendid results the government experts may promise him, he does not necessarily want to risk his carefully hoarded cash, nor does he want to borrow from the village money-lender who charges high rates of interest.

The government of India also realises that the farmer is not going to produce more food just because someone in Delhi tells him it is needed. He has got to be assured that it is worth growing, that it will fetch a good price. Too often in the past if he had a crop to take to market, he made the laborious journey only to find that prices were too low, and he might as well have stayed at home. He was even more discouraged when he learned of the high prices the same crops were fetching in the towns—so high that the underfed people he had been asked to help could not afford to buy them. It was enough to turn him back to his village in despair, back to his traditional ways of unproductive farming.

The old ways may seem less trouble to him, the individual farmer, but for India as a whole, with her millions of people to feed, the old ways mean disaster. The government knows it must reorganise the marketing and distribution of food, to make sure the farmer gets a fair price. They know too that better transport and food distribution are essential to get supplies quickly to areas threatened by famine. They know that storage facilities must be improved to prevent the rotting of precious grain, and its loss to the rats and birds which invade the warehouses.

Meanwhile the campaign goes on to persuade people that large families are not necessary to happiness and security. Large and colourful posters in Delhi show harassed parents surrounded by tribes of screaming babies in squalid slums, while equally eye-catching posters show serene families of four peacefully relaxing in neat houses. Health centres and mobile clinics have been set up to reassure people that contraceptive techniques are safe, effective and cheap.

It is obvious that India can only succeed in all these projects if her people can understand and support them. Like all developing countries, she needs not only highly-educated professional people like doctors, lawyers and politicians; she needs com-

A family planning advertisement in Bombay.

Advice on contraception is provided on a railway platform.

petent mechanics and engineers—and she needs ordinary people who can face change without fear.

These changes are already beginning to show. One observer recently commented that in industrial plants furnaces are no longer described as 'hot' or 'cold', but their heat is recorded accurately in degrees centigrade—a small but telling sign of a fundamental change of attitude. It is this change of attitude that is going to change India.

India is only one of the countries struggling with these epic problems. There are many others in Asia, Africa, and South America, where the supply of food is strained to the limit and beyond by the increase of their populations, by drought, by floods, and by war. They are choosing different ways, different political and economic systems to try to find the solution to their problems, and they urgently need help from the wealthier countries, and from the United Nations. How is this help given?

AID

Everyone knows that the United States is a country of immense wealth. This wealth is due partly to her being able to grow more food and produce more goods than she needs, and she has a considerable surplus to export. In the early 1930s many countries, impoverished by the 1914–18 war, could no longer buy these goods; they went to waste, and many American farmers were ruined. Some farmers were paid by the government *not* to grow corn or rear pigs, so that a reasonable market-price could be maintained. The dreadful irony was that, while thousands of American acres were taken out of production, millions of people in other countries lived on the brink of starvation.

The United States government determined that this should never happen again. They decided that their surpluses should be used to help countries devastated by war, and to support the poorer nations of the world, who were trying to fight their way to prosperity. Americans realised that they could no longer live in isolation, that their prosperity as a country depended on a stable world rich enough to buy from them; they realised too that poverty-stricken, hungry people were all the more likely to be converted to Communism—a political system they detest.

Their scheme of aid to war-torn Europe—the Marshall Plan—broadened in the 1950s to include many Asian and African countries, and in 1954 the Agricultural Trade Development and Assistance Act, or Public Law 480, was passed. It provides for the sale of surplus agricultural commodities to underdeveloped countries and accepts payment in the currency of those countries, not in dollars. It also provides for outright gifts to those countries in times of famine. American aid programmes also provide technical assistance, helping to train engineers and agronomists.

The United States, of course, is not the only government involved, nor are governments the only source of help. Many private firms are investing money in the poorer countries. These firms are building fertiliser plants, exploring for oil and minerals, and building roads, with the hope that these countries as they develop will give a worthwhile return on the investment.

FAO is an agency of the UN. Its purpose is to fight poverty, malnutrition and hunger, and 119 governments contribute money to support it. It also gets funds from the World Bank, the UN Children's Fund and the Freedom from Hunger Campaign, organised in 1960 to link ordinary people with FAO's schemes. It sends money, equipment and experts to help those countries most in need.

Ordinary people are also helping through private organisations like Oxfam which collects and organises the distribution of millions of money gifts, channelling it into the places and projects where it is most needed.

This business of helping underdeveloped countries to feed themselves is a relatively new one; the world is learning new lessons all the time, some of them painful. Many people at first were tempted to think it was all very simple, a straightforward matter of the 'haves' giving to the 'have nots'. But this has proved to be an illusion. The grain surplus of the United States, for instance, will not last much longer, and the poorer countries must rapidly achieve a sufficient increase in their own production. We now realise too that there is no point in supplying expensive machinery like tractors where diesel oil is expensive, where there are no spare parts, few mechanics and no roads. We realise that it is extravagant to send sophisticated earth-moving equipment to countries where there are so many workers who need jobs, and whose labour will cost no more than these imported machines. We still have much to learn about the best way of helping people to fight their own way forward, and to feel that they themselves have worked for their future.

Of course, in times of famine and disaster supplies of food and money are needed and sent immediately. But for the most part the resources of many countries and organisations are being used strategically to set the developing countries on their own independent road to prosperity. So we find experts from FAO advising on irrigation or drainage, fertilisers and pesticides, training Indians, Guatemalans, Thais, and many other peoples to use and develop the techniques they demonstrate. We find them setting up farm mechanisation schools, planning roads, advising governments on credit schemes and cooperatives. We find too that their eyes are fixed firmly on the future, that they are investigating new sources of food, under the seas and in the laboratories. If they are successful we may soon see the development of new processes for making protein cheaply and quickly in factories, and the introduction of new methods of fish farming, to increase fish stocks and make the supplies of fish easier to catch and therefore cheaper.

Perhaps you can begin to see the magnitude of the problem. Perhaps you can begin to see why it has to be tackled on a world scale, and why it needs the good will, determination and money, not only of the people in the developing countries, but also of those who are more fortunate, like ourselves.

FOLLOW-UP WORK

Make a study of one area that practises subsistence farming.

Where are the headquarters of FAO? How is it organised? Find out what FAO is doing in one underdeveloped area.

What diseases are caused by malnutrition? What are their symptoms? How can they be cured?

How much money does your country give to underdeveloped areas? How is it spent? Do you think it is enough?

What are the most common family planning techniques which are most suitable for the developing countries? What are the objections to them?

FURTHER READING

Children of the Developing Countries—a report by the U.N. Children's Fund (T. Nelson, 36 Park Street, London W.1).
Population and Food Supply (H.M. Stationery Office).
Malnutrition and Disease (H.M. Stationery Office).

3 LIVING IN AN INDUSTRIAL AGE

During the second half of the eighteenth century England began on that long process of change that we call the Industrial Revolution. In 1700 most English people lived in the country and made their living from the land; by 1900 most of them were living in cities, and worked in factories and offices.

There was industry in England before 1750, but it was organised on a very small scale. Goods were manufactured either in the workers' own cottages or occasionally in small mills. The only power available other than muscle-power was water. It was difficult to harness and had limited uses, and the machinery it drove was simple, and made of wood.

The great transformation of England's economy in the eighteenth and nineteenth centuries was made possible chiefly by three factors.

First, a new source of power—steam—was harnessed; it was immensely more effective than water-power. It could move heavier loads and drive more and bigger machines at a much faster rate.

Secondly, new processes of iron smelting were discovered which made possible the construction of machinery and engines that were tough enough to be driven by the steam, which would have smashed the old wooden machinery to bits.

The British Industrial Revolution brought prosperity; but it also brought suffering, especially in the early years. This is an illustration from the Mining Report of 1842 showing a child harnessed to a heavy truck.

Thirdly, there was money to pay for it all. England's agriculture and trade were highly profitable. Land-owners and merchants had capital to invest in the new developments, to build the factories, mines, ports and railways that made England's industrial expansion possible.

England was the first country to become industrialised, but she was quickly followed by others—Germany, the United States and Japan. The process is still going on today throughout Europe, South America, Africa and Asia.

To most people industrialisation means progress. It has brought greater wealth and therefore greater influence in the world. It has meant shops full of goods, and cash to spend on them; it has meant not being stuck in one village for the whole of one's lifetime; and it has brought the promise of good hospitals and schools, and of reliable services—electricity, transport, police, sanitation.

PROBLEMS OF INDUSTRIAL DEVELOPMENT

But if you have studied the British Industrial Revolution you will know that there was another side to the picture—long hours of work, low wages, child labour, dangerous machinery. The people who moved into the cities to work in the new factories found dark streets crammed with meanly built houses, blackened by soot from factory chimneys. Nor were they allowed at first to combine together in trade unions to fight for better conditions. For them the changes brought little benefit and much suffering.

But, of course, things did get better. The workers struggled hard and intelligently to improve their lot, and once the great industrial changes were under way, men of

The people . . . found dark streets crowded with meanly built houses.

A mass meeting of London dockers. In most industrial countries workers have the right to form unions to fight for good wages and working conditions.

influence and wealth, including some factory owners, began to work for reform. The government began to recognise that they had some responsibility in the matter and could not just leave the problems to settle themselves. Hours of work were shortened, safety regulations introduced, Trade Unions recognised, and by 1900 millions of people were beginning to enjoy some of the fruits of their country's increasing prosperity. They could afford to buy the cheap factory-produced goods that 150 years before had been made by hand and were therefore far too costly. The growth of the railways meant cheaper fares and the possibility of an occasional day out in the country or at the seaside. Children could go to school and, if they were really clever, win a scholarship to a university. As time went on the growing wealth of the nation came to benefit more and more of its people, with enough surplus wealth to provide an ever increasing measure of welfare for the poor, the sick and the un-employed.

This has been the pattern not just for Britain but for the other industrial countries.

The changes have never been easy. They have been accompanied, and still are, by hardships, disappointments, sometimes by violence; but in the end developing wealth means higher living standards and greater opportunities.

In countries like the United States, Britain and Germany, many of the old problems have been resolved. Living standards are high, and recent developments in science and technology offer prospects of even greater comfort and material wealth. How different, we may think, from the countries who are still struggling for a foothold in the modern world, where life is so hard and so uncertain.

But life in the richer industrial nations is not without its problems and its dangers. They are different from those of the less developed countries certainly, but they can be just as worrying, and just as difficult to solve.

A peasant living in a largely agricultural country may not have money to buy his family expensive imported goods like television sets and cars, or even shoes. But he does control his own food supply—because he grows it himself. This gives him a certain degree of independence and security.

The worker in an industrial country is on the face of it, much better off. He has more furniture, a more varied diet, and can even perhaps afford to run a car. But in some ways he is at a disadvantage. He no longer grows the food his family needs—he has to buy it. He gets the cash to pay for it by selling his skill to an employer. If he can no longer sell his manpower, he is out of a job and his food supplies, his house, his car, even the health of his family is immediately threatened.

An industrial country is especially vulnerable to the ups and downs of world trade. If the raw materials on which industry depends are impeded in any way—as were for instance the supplies of raw cotton to the Lancashire mills by the American Civil War—then the workers in that industry suffer. If a country is spending too much on imports and decides to cut them down, then foreign factories find their order books less full, their profits are slashed, and workers declared redundant. This can happen in any country which earns money from exports, whether of food, raw materials, or manufactured goods. One well-known example may help to show more clearly how a trade depression comes about and how the workers are affected.

THE DEPRESSION

After the 1914–18 war there was in Great Britain a short period of confidence, as soldiers came back to their jobs and industry re-geared itself to peace-time trade. It was not to last. Countries impoverished by the war could no longer buy large quantities of the traditional British products like coal, textiles, ships, and machine tools. Moreover, other European nations were now developing their own industries and becoming serious competitors in markets which Britain had dominated for so long.

Because of the war there was little money available to develop new industries, to provide new jobs for the men who were now thrown out of work in the mines, textile mills and shipyards. A particular industry usually concentrates in a certain

Unemployed men queuing outside a Labour Exchange during the depression.

area, near to its sources of raw materials or to the ports from which its products are exported. If you lived in one of these areas when your particular industry was hit by depression, there was very little chance of switching to some other job. Whole towns, whole regions, became 'depressed areas'.

There were jobs available in London and the South East, but finding a job there was by no means certain, and the risks and expense of moving often seemed too great. The unemployed worker usually preferred to stay where he was, and hope that the factory or shipyard that had given him work in the past would one day open up again.

Tragically, every succeeding year saw that prospect further and further away. The international trade depression, which was by now worldwide, grew worse after the 1929 Wall Street crash and the collapse of American finance. The slump that followed was of terrifying proportions. The total number of men unemployed in the United States rose from 3 million in 1930 to 12 to 15 million in 1933, and their sufferings were sharpened by the lack of any adequate government welfare schemes to help them.

We have already seen how industrial nations are linked together by their trade. Prosperity in one country means full order books in another. In the same way the effects of depression and unemployment never remain isolated within one country —they spread also to that country's trading partners.

Austria, Germany, Great Britain, France, Latin America, were all affected by the United States' misfortune. It was the final blow to the hopes of Britain's unemployed. Even more factories, shipyards and mills were closed. George Orwell wrote in *The Road to Wigan Pier*: 'I remember the shock of astonishment it gave me when I first mingled with tramps and beggars to find that a fair proportion, perhaps a quarter of these beings, were decent young miners and cotton workers, gazing at their

Unemployed workers from the town of Jarrow, marching to London to make the government and the public realize their desperate need for work.

destiny with the same sort of dumb amazement as an animal in a trap. They simply could not understand what was happening to them. They had been brought up to work and behold! it seemed as if they were never going to have the chance of working again.'

By 1933 there were three million unemployed in Britain. Unlike the United States, the government in Britain paid unemployment relief to people without jobs, but in the 1930s 'the dole' for a married man with two children was under 30s. a week—not much even in those days to provide the right sort of food for a family. They relied more and more on starchy, filling food, like bread and potatoes. There was little chance of keeping children at school after 14 for a better education. They had to help support their families; often they too went straight from school on to the dole. In the great 'hunger marches' thousands of unemployed men from Jarrow and South Wales marched to London to plead for work, but although they aroused much compassion, they had little effect.

Ironically, the plight of the unemployed in Britain was only eased when Europe began to prepare once more for war in the late thirties.

Since that time the world's bankers, industrialists and economists have reached a greater understanding of the causes of economic depression, and governments are careful to avoid any action that would trigger off the sort of world unemployment that shadowed the twenties and thirties.

INDUSTRIAL CONFLICT

Yet unemployment still occurs, sometimes as a result of a country's economic difficulties, sometimes because of the introduction of more efficient techniques which can make workers redundant.

In many industrial countries the knowledge of what unemployment can mean over-shadows the relationship between the management of an industry and its employees.

If an industrial country wants to stay prosperous and successful in the modern world it has to be efficient. It has to produce goods as cheaply as possible in order to compete in the world market, and it has to deliver its goods quickly and punctually, or else it loses the chance of further orders. Yet very often the pursuit of efficiency seems to the worker to benefit everyone but himself. Sometimes he will see the small factory where he has worked for years, where he knows the management personally, and where he can sense his own value, taken over by a bigger firm in the interests of progress. He may feel dwarfed by the bigger organisation.

The fear of losing their jobs explains many of the incidents we read about where workers resist with obstinacy any attempt to introduce efficiency-experts into a factory, or to put one man instead of two in charge of a diesel engine, or to allow men in one trade to transfer to the work of another.

The executives and managers of the factory have their problems too. Many of them

Modern factories and offices often provide excellent conditions; even so workers sometimes find the atmosphere impersonal and the jobs repetitive.

thrive in the stimulating atmosphere of a big go-ahead organisation, but there are many who feel the same dislike of working in an impersonal atmosphere as the man on the shop floor.

They often see their long-term planning, their hopes for new business threatened by the workers' resistance to measures they consider essential to the industry's survival. They see their work threatened by disputes and by strikes which paralyse not only one factory but a whole industry.

In many countries there are firms which have made great advances in solving this problem of cooperation between the two sides of industry. They have made contact between shop stewards and management representatives easier, so that disputes can be settled before they escalate into strikes. Considerable care is taken to see that working conditions are pleasant. Many organisations spend time and money on seeing that welfare services are large enough and efficient enough to give the workers the same personal attention that they enjoyed in smaller factories. Some managements take care to explain their policies and their aims to their workers; sometimes profit sharing schemes have been introduced to give the worker an incentive to feel that his firm's success is his too.

These firms are pioneers in trying to achieve the cooperation between all the people on whose differing skills the success of modern industry depends. But there is still much to be done before the sources of industrial conflict are removed.

LIVING IN A CITY

Men have lived in cities for over 5,000 years. The towns of Mesopotamia, Egypt, Greece, Rome, and of Mediaeval Europe, grew up usually as trade developed, providing meeting places for the exchange of goods and centres of record keeping and administration. Some of those towns are now in ruins, or have disappeared altogether; some, like London, Athens and Lyons, are still important today. They were rarely large—Rome at its biggest had a population of 200,000 people; Babylon had about 80,000 people—and only a small proportion of a country's population lived in these cities.

Today we have a completely different situation. As many as 80 per cent of all Britons and 70 per cent of all Americans live in cities, and migration to them is increasing

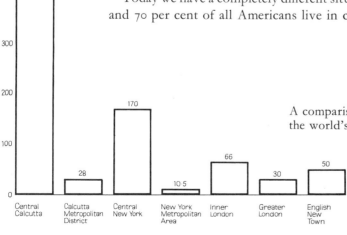

A comparison of the densities of population in some of the world's major cities.

Many Indian peasants coming to Calcutta in search of a better life find conditions like this.

all over the world. Many modern cities are enormous—Greater London 10 million people, Calcutta 7 million people—living in closely packed conditions. According to one American census 53 per cent of the nation's population is concentrated on 0.7 per cent of the nation's land.

These vast cities, which are a feature of most industrial countries, have obvious advantages. They offer their inhabitants a wide choice of jobs, and the chance to move easily from one to another. Rail and road services can bring in raw materials easily, and can despatch vast quantities of products equally swiftly. Banks, offices, warehouses and shops are obviously most useful when they are near to the industries which supply them with business. Hospitals, cinemas, schools, theatres, recreation parks, help to make life safer, easier, and more enjoyable. Many people enjoy living in large towns. They welcome the bustle, the excitement, the stimulus. They like the opportunity for work and for leisure that a big city offers.

But there are many city dwellers who are not so happy; and there are many officials who find the job of running a modern city an almost impossible task.

Perhaps the problem is seen at its worst in the newly developing countries in the throes of their industrial revolutions, where the accommodation and services of the fast growing cities are stretched beyond comfort and safety by their rapidly expanding

Calcutta is now so overcrowded that 100,000 people sleep on the streets.

populations. A particularly dramatic example of the difficulties of such a city are to be found in Calcutta in India.

Calcutta's docks handle 25 per cent of all India's imports and 42 per cent of her exports. It lies close to the great coal and iron deposits of West Bengal. Obviously it is a city already important and destined to see the size of its trade, its businesses, its wealth, grow even greater. But unfortunately it is surrounded by pitifully poor rural areas, and Calcutta is now a city of 7 million people crowded into 400 square miles. Human beings are not easy to control, particularly when their families are starving, and country people have flocked into Calcutta before there was the work to support them or the houses to settle in.

Buildings are congested and inadequate. More than three quarters of the population of the city of Calcutta live in slums. More than 57 per cent of families have only one room to live in. In the slum areas it is estimated that there is one water tap to 25 to 30 people—one lavatory to 23.

Great efforts are made to keep the insides of these houses clean, however poor they are, but the sanitation authorities have been completely overwhelmed by the density of settlement. Garbage is dumped anywhere and there is no stated time for the collection of refuse. Water supplies are overstrained, and hundreds of thousands of people are driven to drink the unfiltered water intended for cleaning the streets and flushing lavatories. Disease here is a constant threat, as it is in all crowded cities.

The traffic problem in Calcutta is appalling. On an average day 50,000 pedestrians and 30,000 vehicles cross the Hawral bridge. There are never enough buses, and when work is found, it often means hours of queueing for transport, or a long exhausting journey on foot.

Food supplies are overstrained too. The peasant coming to Calcutta in search of new opportunities finds food scarce and prices high. Even when he finds a job, his family are no better fed in the city than they were when they lived off the land.

Calcutta is, of course, an extreme example, but however rich a country is, however advanced industrially, there is still the problem of matching housing and services to the demand of ever-increasing numbers.

Whether your home is a modern flat or an old terrace house, town life brings stress and discomfort as well as opportunity.

Life in a New Town is healthier, often happier, but New Towns have new problems.

New York, for instance, is the largest city in the richest nation in the world, yet for all its wealth it is short of water, its air is badly polluted, and garbage often lies uncollected in the streets. Britain is a country with perhaps the longest experience of providing housing for an expanding society, yet her housing shortage still remains her major social problem. Moreover, all industrial cities in whatever continent suffer from traffic congestion and from noise.

All these problems lead to stress, to discomfort, to irritation. It is not surprising that mental illness is an occupational risk of city life, and the incidence of violence and crime is much higher in urban than in rural areas. Those who can afford to move out of the centre to the fresher air of the suburbs have a chance of avoiding the worst effects of city life, but relatively few can afford to.

NEW TOWNS

Often in the last 20 years governments have built complete new towns, and have tried hard to avoid the pitfalls of the old overcrowded cities. Great care has been taken to see that enough work of the right sort was available for the workers who moved there. Factories and houses were built together. Churches, hospitals, schools, open spaces, and houses designed by intelligent architects were planned with great care to offer the new town residents the very best chance of building a happy community. For many people it worked—they enjoyed and still enjoy the cleanness, the

44

nearness to the country, the chance to have a garden of their own. But the new towns still have their problems. People living in the new towns are physically healthier, but mental stress (and therefore the suicide rate and dependence on drugs) is on the increase. Many families find the removal from areas in which they have grown up too disturbing. They feel cut off from their large family groups, particularly from their older relatives who sustained and helped them in all kinds of ways. Often too their possession of new houses coupled with the pressure of television-advertising leads to families committing themselves to over-ambitious hire purchase payments, thus adding to their anxieties.

The trouble is of course that, even in the New Towns, planning authorities have still not fully come to grips with the situation. Running a happy, prosperous, efficient city or town is an extremely complex, delicate business. It needs highly skilled planning from archi   to provide an environment both
hea   lso needs teachers, sociologists,
psy   ity's needs, and to discover what
con   nd happy lives.

_   hese factors into account, is to be
fou   noco valley of Venezuela. This

Rur   nembers of this city council, no doubt, have found.

project has been bedevilled by the usual problem of rural workers being lured by rumours of new opportunities into a city still unready for them. But there has been a most unusual and exciting collaboration between the Venezuelan corporation who are building Cuidad Guyana, and the Joint Centre for Urban Studies of The Massachusetts Institute of Technology and Harvard University. More and more the successful administration of towns and the creation of new ones will depend on the use of exact, scientific studies of the problems involved.

These are only three of the great issues that those of us living in old and new industrial countries should be aware of. They may be enough to suggest the complexity of the problems that surround us, and to help us realise that only people who are well educated and well balanced can hope to live with them happily. Urban life is in many ways difficult and taxing—sometimes downright unpleasant—but perhaps the exciting opportunities it can bring, the prospects it opens up of a vivid and interesting existence, are even now sufficient compensation. As we come to understand better how to plan and regulate our cities, they could one day become the most successful and exciting form of organisation man has ever devised for himself.

FOLLOW-UP WORK

How many people are unemployed in your country? What provisions are made by your government to help them? What steps is your government taking to create more work for them?

Find out what working conditions are like in your local factories.

When an industrial strike occurs, make a careful study of it. Find out what the causes of the dispute are. When a settlement is reached find out how far the causes of dispute have been removed.

If you live in a town make a list of the advantages you enjoy over country-dwellers.

Try to find out to what extent the traffic-flow has increased in your town during the last ten years. What plans has your local authority made to cope with the increase? How much is it going to cost?

FURTHER READING

Stella Davies, *Living through the Industrial Revolution* (Routledge & Kegan Paul).
Andrew Robertson, *The Trade Unions* (Hamish Hamilton).
J. B. Priestley, *English Journey* (Heinemann).
George Orwell, *The Road to Wigan Pier*.
Walter Greenwood, *Love on the Dole*.
Alan Sillitoe, *Saturday Night and Sunday Morning*.
Rayston Pike, *Human Documents of the Industrial Revolution* (Allen & Unwin).

4 RACE

If man had been the sort of animal that stayed in one territory throughout his life, relationships between people of different race would probably be a lot simpler. But man has not always been content to stay put in one territory. From the dawn of history there have been families, tribes, nations who have been tempted or driven from their original lands, and who have sometimes wandered thousands of miles in search of new homes, new conquests, or new opportunities. Sometimes they were fleeing from oppression, like the Israelites from Egypt; or searching for more fertile land like the Anglo-Saxons who came to Britain from the desolate shores of North-West Europe; or seeking mineral wealth like the people who joined in the Gold Rush to the Yukon. For whatever reason, this constant migration has often led to great discoveries, and to great increases in the world's trade and wealth. It has also created many problems and caused great suffering—encounters and clashes between peoples of differing race involving extraordinary fanaticism and brutality. Too often it has led to the exploitation of people at a primitive stage of development by those who were further advanced and sophisticated.

There are very natural reasons why these encounters between different races lead to explosions of violence.

Man, like many other animals, is easily frightened by anyone moving into his territory, and fear makes him hostile and aggressive.

He needs in the same way to feel part of a herd—a closely knit group—and a group rarely feels so tight and secure as when it is turning against an outsider.

He is often worried by his own puny size and weakness, when compared with his environment or even with other animals; so he finds it reassuring to find others of his species whose different appearance and behaviour-patterns give him an excuse to feel superior.

Lastly and perhaps most important he finds it difficult, if not impossible, to express these feelings and anxieties which are largely unconscious. Because of this men can often be taken by surprise by their feelings of aggression; because of their unexpectedness, they are all the more difficult to control.

There are, too, very real sources of irritation and anxiety when two racial groups meet and try to live together; problems of living space, of employment, of varying patterns of behaviour, of religious practice. They would be difficult enough to sort out anyway, but complicated as they are by all these instinctive prejudices and fears, they become in many cases unbearable.

To understand this, let us examine what has happened in three cases of racial encounter, and see how the tensions have arisen, and how the societies involved have reacted to them.

SOUTH AFRICA

Bartholomew Diaz reached the Cape of Good Hope in 1488, but it was not until 1652 that Jan van Riebeck with three ships of the Dutch East India Company arrived at the Cape and started the migration of Dutch settlers to South Africa. Here was an encounter between completely different races. These first white settlers were Calvinists—of strict Puritan beliefs—who were convinced that they were specially chosen and favoured by God. They had never seen black people before, and because the Hottentots, as they contemptuously called them, spoke an incomprehensible language and showed no wish to work for them, they felt automatically superior, and could only think of the Africans as servants, never as equals. This attitude was scarcely surprising—the seventeenth-century white man had little understanding of how societies had grown up, or of how human beings could develop. They had no conception of how they themselves had once been through a primitive tribal period during their history. The Africans fitted all too clearly into the neat category of 'hewers of wood and drawers of water', described in the Old Testament, which they believed to be the literal truth. They held the belief, common throughout the seventeenth century, that their world was unchanged since its creation, and that the relative backwardness of the African was as permanent as the shape of Table Mountain.

Gradually they pushed further into this promising country. These migrant farmers, or Trekboers, would have been scornful of any thought that they were stealing the Africans' lands. They felt so much more intelligent, so much more competent to make good use of it. When they encountered the Bushmen, the nomadic hunters of the interior, they were furious that these primitive, slightly built black people should dare to defend their territories with poisoned arrows; their reaction was to try to wipe them out completely.

In 1755 the Trekboers reached the Great Fish River, and another encounter between black and white brought further violence. This time the enemy was less easy to deal with. These were the Bantu speaking Africans—their numbers were vast, they were well organised, and they fought desperately for their land in a series of battles—the Kaffir Wars.

The situation was further complicated by another migration—that of the British who, at the end of the Napoleonic Wars, took over control of the Cape. The early British administrators were extremely conservative, and determined opponents of

Boer settlers trekking further into the interior of South Africa.

new ideas. Nevertheless they believed in the rule of law, and that all races in Africa should be equally protected by that law. To the fury of the Boers (the Dutch settlers) these British administrators, when judging legal disputes, were, because of this belief, prepared on occasion to arrive at verdicts supporting the rights of the native Africans rather than the white settlers.

The Boer farmer was living in difficult and often dangerous frontier conditions, and he found this kind of impartial justice extremely irritating. Even more distasteful to him was the attitude of the English missionaries, who defended the rights of the Africans and even believed that they could one day become educated and responsible. The Boers were equally devout Christians, but with very different interpretations of Christianity. They often treated their African slaves with care and affection, but always paternally, as fathers to children, and could never conceive that one day the children might grow up and be independent of them.

A clash of interests had already led to war between the black and white races. Now there was an added conflict—that between the policies of the two white nations. In the end many Boer farmers, frustrated beyond endurance by what they considered wrong-headed British policies, decided to move their homes once more and trek

C

49

with their families into new territories, which were to become three new independent Provinces. Here they could feel free to organise their lives, and their African labour, in the way they considered realistic.

There was undoubtedly by this time great resentment among the Boers against the policies of the British administration. There were jealousies and conflicts between the two white races which ultimately led to the Boer War of 1889–1902. Despite all this, the feelings towards the African of all the white farmers, whether they were Afrikaans or British, was very much the same—their feelings of superiority were reinforced by the need for cheap labour on their farms and later in the gold and diamond mines. They were convinced that the white man must be the boss not just until the Africans became educated to European standards (they denied that this was possible), but for good.

This seemed good sense to most white people. To the Afrikaaner it was also a matter of deep religious conviction, for the Dutch Reformed Church to which he belonged still proclaimed, as it had in the seventeenth century, that the white man had been appointed by God to rule over the black.

In 1913 an alliance of English and Afrikaans-speaking whites, under the leadership of Louis Botha, a former Boer General, formed the government of South Africa. Those die-hard Afrikaaners who were unwilling to compromise with the English, against whom they had fought so bitterly, formed an opposition to this government and called themselves the Nationalist party. The Government, although moderate and well-meaning, like most of the white South Africans it represented, still had an outlook dominated by past experiences. Its members could still only think of the Africans as a backward race, who had done nothing to develop the vast resources of their native country. They could not imagine a South Africa in which the black races played more than a subordinate role. The great task of building a modern, prosperous country was, they felt, a task only the white races could undertake successfully. They decided therefore that no more land was to be sold to Africans outside the territory already reserved for them. It meant, in fact, that the Africans who formed three-quarters of the population were now restricted to one-eighth of the land which they had once felt to be theirs.

In 1924 the National Party—the party of the Afrikaaners—came into power under General Herzog. Here was a man of great integrity and great concern for the welfare of the Africans and of the Coloured people (the descendants of the mixed marriages common in the early history of South Africa). Nevertheless he still thought of them as an irrevocably backward race, and believed that the responsibility for the government of South Africa must always rest with the white races. He took steps to see that the balance of political power rested with them, and he gave the vote to all white men and women however poor or uneducated. By 1932 his laws had had their effect: 39,000 non-white voters, 850,000 white ones!

Moreover his own party, the Nationalists, had temporarily formed an alliance with the Labour party, the party which represented the interests of working men—but only white working men. They were anxious to protect their own jobs, and to keep out any African and Coloured competition. This meant that they too wanted Africans and Coloureds kept firmly in their place as unskilled workers, no matter how capable they might be of further training and education. Laws were passed to close skilled and semi-skilled trades to the Africans and to the many Indians, who by this time had come, as the Afrikaaners and English had once come, in search of new opportunities and wealth.

In 1948 the Nationalist party again came into power, and by this time they had come to believe in a policy of even more rigorous separation between racial groups. This policy was given the name of apartheid (separateness) and the Nationalist Party under Dr Malan (1948–55), Mr Strijdom (1955–58) and Dr Verwoerd (1958–66) passed a series of laws which tried to impose this separation as quickly as possible.

Inconveniently for the South African government, progress and development in South Africa has always been dependent on African manpower! If all Africans lived solely in the specially reserved areas known as Bantustans, that manpower would vanish, and trade and industry would come to a halt. Some Africans therefore have to be allowed in to the towns, but only to work; they are made to live in native areas specially allotted and often miles away from their jobs.

Because the African is seen as different and separate, his education is also planned differently. Dr Verwoerd himself claimed: 'There is no place for the Native in the

What apartheid—separate development can mean—separate paths across a bridge in Capetown.

European community above the level of certain forms of labour. . . . It is of no avail for him to receive a training which has as its aim absorption in the European community.'

Schools run by missionary societies, like Father Trevor Huddleston's school in Capetown, which once provided a European-style education for African children, have been closed down. The government feels that education should be designed to preserve the differences between the races, and that as far as possible Africans should be taught in their own language, only those subjects which would be of use in the range of jobs available to them.

Other laws have ensured more and more rigid separateness in every aspect of life, however trivial. Black and white people are not allowed to inter-marry, to sit together in buses or on park benches. There are different queues at the post offices, and separate areas on the beaches. They must even enter railway stations at separate entrances.

To the men who shape the policy all this seems good logic and good sense. 'If you reduce the number of points of contact to the minimum, you reduce the possibility of friction. Contact brings about friction and friction brings about heat and may cause conflagration.' (Dr T. E. Dönges, Minister of the Interior, 1950).

They would argue that their Coloured and African people are well looked after, and that the prosperity and stability of South Africa are in marked contrast to the bloodshed and chaos of independent African states like the Congo and Nigeria.

There are many people in South Africa, black and white, who disagree. They would argue that such a rigid policy can only be imposed by increasingly harsh police methods, loss of personal liberty and freedom of speech.

They would claim that the separate education policy means a waste of the intelligence of thousands of Africans who could become the technicians and engineers that a modern South Africa desperately needs.

They would claim that separation, rather than reducing tension, increases bitterness and resentment, and will make bloodshed inevitable.

They ask why, in the attempt to separate the races, Africans always seem to come off badly, getting the least fertile lands, the least attractive parts of the beach. They see Apartheid not as a policy to protect the native peoples but to increase further the wealth and power of the white races of South Africa.

They claim that in a land where the white population is dependent on the black for their labour in homes and farms, in the factories and mines, separate development can never make sense.

THE UNITED STATES OF AMERICA

The people who in the seventeenth century settled in the southern part of the American colonies, found that the land was not suitable for the mixed farming that they had been used to in England. More profit came from large farms or plantations concentrating on one crop that could easily be exchanged for cash or other goods

—usually tobacco and later cotton. These great plantations could not be run by one man or one family with a few hired hands; they needed a plentiful supply of labour. At first white 'indentured servants' were used. These were men, women and children, sometimes convicts, some of whom were persuaded or forced aboard ship and bound to their masters for a term varying from five to seven years.

In 1619 the first Negro slaves from West Africa were brought to the colony of Virginia by a Dutch ship, but for 50 years relatively few Negroes were used. Gradually, however, it became apparent that not only was a Negro slave a better bargain than an indentured servant, in that he remained a slave for life, but he was easier to control, and found the climate more bearable than did the white worker.

The sufferings that were casually, unimaginatively imposed on the African negro, dragged from his land and family to suit the convenience of the white plantation owners, are well known. Herded like cattle into the holds of ships, many did not survive the dangerous crossing.

Appalling as the conditions in the slave ships were, the profits for the slave traders and the plantation owners were great enough to quieten their consciences. By the outbreak of the American Revolution in 1774 there were approximately half a million negro slaves in the colonies, and in five of them—Georgia, North and South Carolina, Virginia, and Maryland—the number of slaves either equalled or exceeded the whites.

This use of slaves brought wealth; it also brought fear and insecurity—the in-

Africans were herded on to the slave ships that were to take them across the Atlantic to the plantations in the Southern States of America.

security of knowing that the prosperity of the southern colonies, later to become the southern states, depended on the labour of these unknown, primitive people. There was always the fear that one day they might become aware of their strength and their numbers and turn against their white masters.

So, as in South Africa, the development of the southern states brought the old mixture of growing dependence on, and often affection for, the negro slaves on the plantations and in the homes of the white southerners, coupled with a growing determination to keep them servile at all costs. Statutes in the 1660s provided that negroes should be slaves for life, and in the years that followed other laws were passed, defining the negroes simply as property, and depriving them of the most elementary rights in the courts. It had been asserted in South Carolina in 1712 that negroes were 'of barbarous, wild, savage natures', and most southerners in the mid-nineteenth century firmly believed that this would be true again of their often docile, cooperative and trusted slaves if there was any attempt to relax the rigid control under which they were kept.

Here too, as in South Africa, we find an alliance between wealthy landowners and poorer white people, to keep the black race firmly in its allotted place. The ordinary yeoman farmer of the southern states, raising and selling his cash crops on a small scale, was increasingly unable to compete with the wealthy plantation-owner, and he and his land were gradually becoming impoverished. Yet his fears of negro competition, of possible negro violence, his feelings of superiority, drove him into throwing his support firmly behind the rich slave owners whose interests dominated southern politics.

The Civil War between the northern and southern states was only partially about slaves, but after the surrender of the southern (Confederate) army at Appomattox, Virginia, on April 9, 1865, the negroes felt convinced that they would now be free to live on equal terms with whites.

For a time the prospect looked good. During the first bitter years after the war, the sudden granting of votes to the negroes led, throughout the southern states, to the formation of secret societies like the Ku Klux Klan and the Knights of the White Camellia, whose aim was to frighten the negro once more into submission; but on the whole the freeing of the slaves did not lead to the violence the white southerners had always feared. Northern visitors to the south in the 1880s were favourably impressed by the easy relationships, and the growing acceptance of the negro in the police force, in the government, and in the street cars.

Unfortunately it did not last. By the end of the nineteenth century anti-negro feeling had once more begun to sway the policies of the southern states legislatures, and because the Federal Government and the Supreme Court did not control them firmly enough, they began to reduce the southern negro to his original inferior status in society.

They introduced voting qualifications, which resulted in very few negroes being able to vote. In Louisiana in 1896 there were 130,000 registered negro voters; in 1904 there were less than 1,350.

'Jim Crow' laws were passed prescribing separate accommodation in street cars and steam boats, in theatres, in mental hospitals, in prisons. Many cities allotted separate residential districts. Many prohibited negro residents altogether. Schools were segregated, and North Carolina and Florida even prescribed different textbooks in the schools.

More frightening to the negro than these laws was the deep hostility which he could sense among white people. In the 1870s and 1880s these fears had been kept firmly in control by the Federal Government in Washington, but now towards the end of the century they were reappearing. In many states mobs began to attack negro quarters of the cities, and negroes were frequently lynched (put to death by a mob) on the flimsiest excuse.

For nearly 300 years this confrontation between white and black was confined to the southern states of America, but after the First World War the situation changed.

The war had led to a great expansion of American industry, yet at the same time had stopped the steady stream of immigrants coming from Europe that had for years helped to provide the vast labour force for American industry.

Many negroes, hard put to it to find a living in the increasingly conservative and backward-looking south, were attracted north by the promise of more and better jobs, and of more freedom. In 1910 only one in ten negroes lived outside the southern states, but by 1960 there would be more negroes outside than in them.

Once again hope was frustrated. 360,000 negroes had served in the army during the war, but they still had not been accepted into American society. In the summer of 1919, 26 race-riots took place, and the worst of these were not in the south at all, but in Chicago, where white mobs seized control of the city, burning negro property and assaulting negroes indiscriminately. White working people, terrified for the safety of their jobs as more and more negro labour became available, banned negro workers from their unions.

By this time many negroes were ready and able to protest, and they had the strong and articulate support of many liberal-minded white Americans. But the American negro was increasingly aware of a dilemma. Should he work for full acceptance in every way by the white community, or should he turn his back on them, reassert his pride in his own race and his solidarity with black races all over the world, and work for a separate development that would give him power and influence in his own right?

The National Association for the Advancement of Coloured People, established in 1910, chose the first course, and they were supported with funds and the devoted work of many white as well as black members.

But despite the work of the NAACP, despite the Federal Government's awareness of the problem, the setting up of university departments to study race relations, and despite the growing prosperity and contentment of many middle class negroes—there was still smouldering hatred and bitterness between white extremists and the negro poor. Time after time their faith in new Presidents and new laws was shattered, and their hopes for dramatic reforms disappointed. After the Second World War,

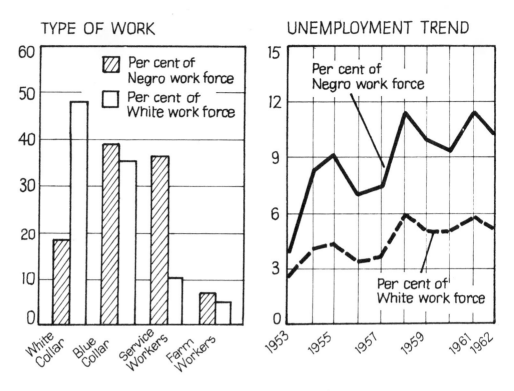

TYPE OF WORK   UNEMPLOYMENT TREND

These two charts show the contrast in main types of employment and the level of unemployment between the white and black working populations of the United States.

millions more negro workers moved north, swamping the already overcrowded
negro districts. Schools and housing were overwhelmed, and living conditions
became more and more unbearable. With the end of the war came a drop in the
demand for labour, and many American negroes in northern cities, already living
in overcrowded conditions and poorly educated, had now to cope with the additional
burden of unemployment. All these problems led to an atmosphere of tension,
irritation and bitterness, in which violence and rebellion are easily triggered off.

The southern negro on his part faced all the old prejudice and refusal to change with
increasing impatience. Especially after the Second World War negro ex-servicemen,
who had served abroad and had been welcomed as equals in many European towns,
were determined to exercise their full rights as American citizens.

President Truman made a Civil Rights programme one of the biggest issues for the
1948 presidential election, and demanded a federal law against lynching, an end to
segregated housing, and a denial of federal aid to any state that refused to give the
negro his full rights under the American constitution.

But there were many Southern Democrats, 'Dixiecrats', in Truman's own party
who were determined opponents of any attempt to end racial segregation, and they
combined with the Republicans to throw out the Civil Rights Bill. Moreover the

separate states of America, particularly in the south, have always resented interference in their affairs by the Federal Government in Washington, and have continually asserted their right to resist any Federal law of which they disapprove.

In 1954 the United States Supreme Court, the body of distinguished judges whose job it is to see that the United States adheres to its written constitution, declared that segregation in American schools was unconstitutional, and stated that arrangements to educate the two races separately were 'inherently unequal'. The southern states were appalled, and did all they could to resist the Supreme Court decision.

In 1957 the negroes of Little Rock, Arkansas, were granted a court order to admit their children to the Central High School, so far reserved for white children. Governor Orval Faubus was not prepared to tolerate this first step towards black and white children being educated together. He ordered out the National Guard to prevent the negro children entering the school, and when he was forbidden to do this a white mob gathered at the school to take over from the Guards.

To millions of people in the United States, Little Rock had been a pretty remote place, but thanks to television confronting them in their own drawing-rooms with pictures of a few nice-looking negro children being kept out of school by hundreds of yelling whites, they were brought smack up against reality. Moreover the United

Teenagers demonstrating against negroes being allowed to enter their schools — Little Rock, Arkansas.

Martin Luther King talking to some of his followers.

States administration knew that those pictures were flashing not only round America but round the whole world. This time there was no chance of letting things drift.

Federal troops were called out to protect nine negro children as they went into the school and, faced with a choice of integrated schools or none at all, white parents at last decided to let the negroes in.

Despite occasional victories like this, many frustrated negroes were more and more coming to believe that only a policy of complete separation between the races could give them the security and opportunities they longed for. Their hopes of peaceful coexistence had been disappointed too many times. The Black Muslim movement which had been founded in 1930 was growing in numbers and in power. Their teaching claims that the Black races were the first civilised people, and that one day —a day of Judgement—the white races will be destroyed and the black people will inherit the earth. The Black Muslim has no wish to integrate with the whites; he wants a separate black republic within the United States, with separate schools and businesses—a policy of apartheid—but this time, in the interests of the black, not the white race.

There was another response, another way open to the desperate negro—Martin Luther King's answer: the Christian one of non-violence. His Southern Christian Leadership Conference organised and financed disciplined, peaceful demonstrations which took place all over the south—'sit-ins' at segregated lunch counters, 'kneel-ins' at segregated churches, 'wade-ins' at segregated beaches, and the famous 'Freedom Rides' by which negroes tried to establish the right, accorded by the Supreme Courts, to use bus terminals and buses hitherto reserved for whites.

These demonstrations, which were organised with great skill, made a considerable impact on opinion not only in the United States but all over the world. Unfortunately within the southern states they intensified white violence, and led to many arrests of negro demonstrators for 'disturbing the peace'.

In 1968 the assassination of Martin Luther King was followed by a funeral in which thousands of people, including the President of the United States, paid tribute to his single-mindedness and steady Christianity. It was also followed by frightening outbreaks of arson and violence in the negro districts of many great cities.

As negro rage and frustration grow, as negro poverty and overcrowding increase, outbursts like this have become almost commonplace in the long hot summers of America that send tempers to flashpoint and make squalor and the feeling of rejection harder to bear.

The assassination of Martin Luther King in 1968 was followed by frightening outbreaks of violence and arson.

Yet where civic leaders have stood firm and upheld federal law, despite threatening noises and even terrorism from extremists, there is some evidence that people are beginning to accept desegregation. More and more people are coming to realise that unless the United States government presses on with its policy of desegregation and its efforts to remedy the social conditions and the ignorance which have bred so much racial violence in the past, the future stability and prosperity of the United States will continue to be in grave jeopardy.

THE JEWS IN GERMANY

Our concern nowadays to prevent racial tension wherever possible is understandable. We live in an age in which racial hatred resulted in probably the greatest act of barbarity in the history of the world—Hitler's treatment of the Jews of Europe.

The Jews have always, since their expulsion from Palestine in the fourth century and their dispersal throughout Europe, been an easy target for persecution. Their intelligence and resource, their willingness to lend money at high rates of interest during a period when usury was forbidden to Christians, often helped them to positions of great wealth. The resulting hostility was inflamed every Easter when the story of the Crucifixion was told.

It was comforting for a peasant, horrified by the story of Jesus's suffering, to feel

Hitler was able to convince many Germans that their economic troubles were caused by Jews.

1945. German civilians are made to see the results of Hitler's policy—in front of them is a lorry piled high with the bodies of concentration camp victims.

he did not need to share the guilt, that he could heap it all on to the Jews, forgetting that Jesus himself was one.

It was tempting to blame one's own misfortune on a Jew rather than on one's oneself, easier for an uneducated man to kill a Jew than to try and understand the real reasons for his poverty.

The history of Christianity is flawed by the sickening cruelty of the pogroms—race riots—when Jewish property was burned and Jewish families were beaten and slaughtered.

Adolf Hitler, friendless, hungry, and without a job, living in Vienna before the First World War, reading anti-Jewish pamphlets, probably felt this sense of relief on finding that here was a simple explanation of all his failure and inadequacy—it could all be blamed on the Jews. He later found it easy to convince the German people, humiliated by defeat and depressed by economic chaos after the First World War. Their society, he told them, was riddled with corruption because of the Jews who were plotting to dominate Europe.

When Hitler came to power as Fuehrer in 1933, this hatred of the Jews was given full rein. Jews were forbidden to marry Gentiles, they were deprived of official posts, and any lout looking for amusement could beat up a Jew, or wreck his business, without fear of punishment.

After the assassination of a German official in Paris by a young Polish Jew, Germany was swept by a wave of Anti-Semitism, and Hitler's policy became more savage. He now began to plan 'The Final Solution' to the Jewish Problem—complete extermination. Jewish property was burned and looted and the Jews were taken into 'protective custody'—imprisoned in concentration camps. Here the Jews, together with other prisoners who had dared to criticise Hitler's regime, were used as a vast slave labour force. The heads of the camps were ordered to get every ounce of use from their prisoners by flogging and torture, and certain categories of prisoners were classified as suitable, in the words of the official documents, 'to be worked to death'.

These prisoners were joined by millions more Jews from all over Europe as Hitler extended his rule during the Second World War. In the end most of them were herded on cattle trucks and transported to extermination camps, like Auschwitz in Poland. In these camps Hitler's plan for a 'Final Solution' was put into effect; men, women and children were driven into gas chambers, their bodies shovelled into vast incinerators. By 1945, between 5 and 6 million Jews had been killed, and death came to them only after unimaginable suffering of mind and body.

The staffs of the extermination-camps had been conditioned over a long period by Hitler's propaganda to think of Jewish people as dangerous sub-human creatures. They could kill them easily because they felt no link with them, no sympathy. Their crimes stand to remind us that all of us, whatever our nation or race, are capable of evil, especially when our instinctive suspicions and fears are fostered and used by an irresponsible government.

They remind us too that we need to be honest about our own prejudice against other racial groups.

We need to recognise prejudice in order to overcome it, and try, under the governments we elect, to create the kind of society which gives it no chance to take root.

FOLLOW-UP WORK

Do you feel hostility to any racial group? What do you think are the reasons for this hostility?

Make a collection of newspaper cuttings showing 'apartheid' at work.

What are 'frontier conditions'? Where else have they existed? Why do frontiersmen tend to be suspicious of government laws?

Try to find in the newspaper examples of incidents showing southern states' dislike of Federal interference.

Find out about the resistance movement in Germany which opposed Hitler's ideas and policies.

Find examples from newspapers of present-day anti-semitism among:
    (a) private people,
    (b) governments.

FURTHER READING

H. H. Swift, *The Railroad to Freedom* (Bodley Head).
Albert Luthuli, *Let My People Go* (Collins).
Alan Paton, *Cry the Beloved Country*.
Mary Benson, *The African Patriots* (Faber and Faber).
Antony Sampson, *Common Sense about Africa* (Gollancz).
Katharine Savage, *The Story of Africa* (Bodley Head).
Janet Harris, *The Long Freedom Road*. (The Civil Rights Story). (Constable).
Philip Mason, *Common Sense about Race* (Gollancz).
Trevor Huddleston, *Nought for your Comfort* (Collins).
The Bishop of Johannesburg, *Shooting at Sharpeville* (Gollancz).
S. K. Ruck, *The West Indian comes to England* (Routledge & Kegan Paul).
Charity Blackstock, *Wednesday's Children* (Hutchinson).

5 VIOLENCE AND THE USE OF FORCE

Man has been able to survive and develop, to build great civilisations, largely because of an ability that sets him apart from all other animal species—he can make and use tools.

This distinctive aptitude has given him great power, but it is a power that can be used to destroy as well as to build. Over the centuries, as tools have become more sophisticated and elaborate, so have weapons. We have now reached a point where we have been so successful and ingenious in our development of tools of destruction, that we are capable not only of destroying an army or a nation, but all life on this planet.

We have shown great skill and intelligence in developing these terrifying weapons; the great question now is whether we can show enough wisdom to build a world in which they will no longer be needed.

We have to face another problem, in its way just as serious. Violence of a crude primitive kind still exists, even in the most civilised societies. We seem nowadays to be threatened by more and more riots and disturbances, in which the weapons are as old as man himself—sticks, stones, hands and feet. However simple the weapons, violence still hurts, still frightens, still has the power to intimidate, and to disturb the peace of society.

If we are ever to control our urge to violence, we must first understand its causes. If we are ever to prevent wars, we must know when and why they are likely to happen; if we are ever to see an end to personal and mob violence, we must understand the sort of situations that are likely to trigger it off. By studying a number of instances in the history of this century, characterised by the use of force, we shall find no easy answers to the problems; but we may see more clearly the essence of it, and how urgent the need for a solution.

VIOLENCE IN DEFENCE OF TERRITORY: THE SOVIET UNION AGAINST NAZI GERMANY

One of our most powerful instincts, deriving from our animal ancestors, is the urge to protect the territory we live in. The most desperate battles are fought, the most

64

heroic sacrifices are made when men feel their homes threatened. Indeed many people feel that violence used in their defence is entirely justified.

A most dramatic example of this in the twentieth century was the Russians' defence of their homeland against Nazi Germany during the Second World War.

On 18 December 1940, Hitler, irritated by Stalin's refusal to become a subservient ally, and fearing that Russia might in the end support Britain, decided to launch 'Operation Barbarossa'—the invasion of Russia. He anticipated little difficulty in defeating the Red Army, and confidently made detailed plans for the occupation of Russian territory.

Stalin had no wish to see his country embroiled in a costly war, and up to the last moment tried to ignore the threat that was building up, a threat of which he was repeatedly warned by British, American, and Soviet intelligence. On 13 June 1941 he even went so far as to issue a public statement ridiculing the rumours that German troops were massing on the frontiers—an ostrich-like attitude which is one of the most typical human responses to the threat of violence: pretend it isn't there and it might go away!

In the early hours of 22 June 1941, however, those very German troops whose presence Stalin had so scornfully denied crossed the frontier, and most of the Soviet air force was destroyed on the ground. A few weeks later it looked as though Hitler's hopes of a quick victory would be fulfilled, as his armies rolled inexorably on. By November German patrols were in the suburbs of Moscow.

And yet Moscow never fell. The tide of war was turned by the grim determination

Violence on the streets.

of a people fighting for their homeland. This spirit not only stiffened the morale of the Russian forces, it made the ordinary citizens of towns like Leningrad and Stalingrad hold out in the most appalling conditions rather than surrender to the invading army.

Probably the most epic courage was shown by the Russians living in territory already occupied by the Germans. They refused to acknowledge defeat, and formed themselves into 'partisan' units to carry on the fight 'underground'. Every partisan fighter, man or woman, took a vow 'to take revenge on the enemy cruelly, tirelessly, and without mercy . . . to perish in fierce combat with the enemy rather than surrender my family and all my people to fascist slavery.' They blew up railway tracks, burned down bridges, and killed any German they could find. The savage reprisals imposed by the Germans served only to make them more determined. By the middle of 1942 it is estimated that these self-organised guerilla groups were pinning down over 10 per cent of Hitler's forces.

However brilliant the Russian generals, however well-organised their campaigns, the story of the Russian fight against Germany is the story of ordinary men driven by their instinct for territory to use any means at their disposal, even if it involved the sacrifice of their own lives, to hold on to it. To them the use of violence needed no justification; it was simply a matter of survival.

VIOLENCE OF DESPAIR: THE WARSAW GHETTO

Sometimes human beings are faced with situations so hopeless that they despair of there being any end to their suffering, and resolve on violent action, knowing that it will almost certainly cause their death.

When Hitler occupied his European conquests, he imposed on them, just as he had on Germany, the policy of imprisoning and killing the Jews. The Jews who lived in the ghettoes of Warsaw, in Poland, knew very well what their fate was likely to be. Knowing the horrors that awaited them and their families they decided on a showdown. On 18 January 1943, a group of Jewish workers selected for deportation to German concentration-camps was being marched away when several of them pulled out guns and fired at their captors. Many Jews were killed in the struggle that followed but others escaped and fled back to their homes. The whole Jewish population now banded together, determined to resist arrest. Although vastly outnumbered, they organised themselves into combat groups, to fight to the death.

The Nazi authorities, furious at this upset to their plans, entered the ghetto with armoured cars. For five weeks the Jews fought savagely, from their houses, from underground shelters, and from the sewers. As the German commander wrote in a despatch: 'Over and over again we observed that Jews, despite the danger of being burned alive, were prepared to return to the flames rather than be caught by us.' In the end, of course, the greater force prevailed. The surviving Jews were deported, the ghetto-area razed to the ground, and all sewer and cellar openings sealed off. The rebellion achieved nothing for the Jews, nor was it expected to, except the chance of death in combat rather than in the gas-chamber, and the sheer animal satisfaction of a last desperate act of defiance against forces they knew to be overwhelming.

REVOLUTIONARY VIOLENCE: CUBA

Sometimes, when men are angered by a government they consider unjust and incompetent, they become frustrated by the failure of their peaceful attempts to change the government or its policies. When this happens, they are likely to turn from peaceful to violent action, and try, sometimes by the assassination of one man, sometimes by a military take-over (a coup d'état), to overthrow the government of which they disapprove.

Cuba, like many other Latin American countries, was for 300 years part of the Spanish Empire. When Cuba achieved her independence at the beginning of the twentieth century she was suffering, like the other newly-liberated Latin American countries, from the effects of many years of foreign rule. The Spanish government had been absolutist, holding power closely in its own hands, and allowing the local population no share in public affairs. When independence came there was little possibility of establishing a democratic government, one in which the people could take part.

Cuba, moreover, was a land with poor communications. Her peasants were often isolated in remote areas, and they would have found it difficult to take an interest in government even if they had been sufficiently literate to do so. This meant that the power of government was concentrated in the hands of a minority of landowners and military leaders. From 1933 to 1952 Cuba was ruled by a dictator, Fulgencio Batista, whose rule was particularly corrupt and brutal.

Harsh dictatorial rule usually results in discontent, a discontent which, because of the dictator's refusal to listen to criticism and to give up any of his powers, often results in bloodshed and revolution.

In Cuba's case the dissatisfaction with Batista was further inflamed by anger at Cuba's poverty. Spain had regarded Cuba as a source of raw materials, and as a market for Spanish goods. Consequently Cuba, like Spain's other Latin-American possessions, had not been allowed to develop her resources for her own benefit. This meant that although Cuba became independent of Spain in the matter of government, that is *politically*, she was not yet able to stand on her own feet *economically*. She was still heavily dependent on imports from abroad, and no one in Cuba had sufficient capital to invest in building new sources of wealth. Cuba was therefore dependent on foreign investors, who were naturally only interested in the production of the crops that they themselves needed. Consequently, the sugar industry became the great prop of the Cuban economy, accounting for more than four-fifths of her exports. It was an industry run entirely for one market, the United States, and American businessmen were prepared to invest heavily in Cuba to ensure that their supplies of raw sugar were efficiently produced. American money made possible the development of

Cuba's power-supplies, roads and railways, and telecommunications. Because of this heavy American investment, Cuba acquired the superficial appearance of a thriving go-ahead country with busy towns, impressive buildings, and a number of extremely wealthy people.

Most Cubans, however, resented their economic dependence on American business. They knew that the sugar industry, while bringing prosperity to the small wealthy section of the community, did not favour the peasants who worked on the plantations. The production of sugar is confined to certain seasons of the year, and during the off-season most of the workers were therefore unemployed, and the rural areas remained poor and backward. There were many other Latin-American countries where the peasants were as poor, even poorer, but nowhere was there such a gap between rich and poor as in Cuba. The wealth of the few made the poverty of the many seem the more unjust.

This bitter resentment led to mounting criticism, which led in turn to Batista's

Demonstrators in Havana celebrating the success of the Castro revolution.

government becoming even harsher and more brutal in its efforts to stamp out all signs of opposition. It was this intensified repression that provided the spark to kindle the discontent which had been smouldering for so many years.

Fidel Castro, a lawyer who had been educated at Havana University, was the leader whose personality was to help weld this resentment into an organised revolutionary force. He believed, with many others, that all hope of a peaceful change of government was at an end and that the time for violence had arrived. In July 1953 he organised an attack on a barracks. He was caught and was sentenced to 15 years' imprisonment, but was fortunate to be released only two years later. In 1956 he organised an invasion of Cuba from Mexico, but was defeated by Batista's troops and forced to retreat into the mountains.

Realising that the efforts of his small army were useless against Batista's entrenched regime, he bided his time. The next two years he spent in hiding to build up a network of secret opposition groups in cities all over Cuba. Their work, and Batista's increasing severity, ensured that when Castro was ready to strike again, effective government resistance had already been undermined. In January 1959 the Batista regime was overthrown, and Castro came to power as the head of a radical socialist government which has since transformed Cuban life, and become a focus for revolutionary activity throughout Latin America.

THE VIOLENCE OF FRUSTRATION: STUDENT REVOLT

The last few years have seen frequent protest-meetings, marches, and sit-ins by students all over the world. They have often led to violent clashes between students and police—in some instances of a ferocity that has surprised and shocked the public. Why do they happen?

Many young people at universities all over the world are appalled by the wars and injustice, the suffering and poverty they see around them. They feel that their society not only tolerates these evils but seems actively to support them, and must therefore be corrupt, out of date and evil. Some students want to shock the public simply into realising this for themselves and so strengthen existing movements for reform, others aim at abolishing present political and economic systems, and building what they believe to be a more worthwhile order to take their place.

French students, in addition to this general disenchantment and anger with the world as they see it, have had a number of specific grievances about conditions within their universities.

The passing of the French 'Baccalauréat' examination gives the automatic right to enter university without further examination, and consequently the universities in France are greatly overcrowded. Accommodation is stretched beyond the point of even basic comfort, and there is little opportunity for students to get to know their lecturers, or to go to them for help. Because there are so many students, there are thousands of men and women leaving universities every year with perfectly good degrees, but little prospect of a suitable job.

French students building a barricade during the Paris riots in 1968.

In 1964 a new extension to the University of the Sorbonne was opened at Nanterre, a suburb of Paris. But by 1968 the number of students had leapt to 11,000 and the students claimed that the accommodation was totally inadequate, and that the teaching was still impersonal and largely irrelevant.

On 26 January there was a protest demonstration by 40 students at Nanterre. The authorities called in the police, with the result that hundreds more students, infuriated by the police intervention, joined the demonstration.

The arrest of the ring leaders, including Danny Cohn Bendit—one of the key personalities—led to much greater disturbances in Paris itself. Police were summoned to clear four hundred student demonstrators from the Sorbonne on 3 May, and this time police-intervention escalated the demonstration into weeks of street fighting. Barricades were built, pneumatic drills used to tear up paving stones, tyres were slashed, and home-made petrol bombs thrown at armoured cars. On 24 May an attempt was made to burn down the Paris Stock Exchange, which many students saw as a symbol of the rottenness and materialism of their society. The police fought back with a brutality that disturbed many eye-witnesses, who had little sympathy with either the behaviour or aims of the students, and *The Times* correspondent commented: 'These boys and girls may not have known what they were fighting for, but they certainly fought with the energy of despair.'

VIOLENCE AMONG NATIONS: THE CUBA CRISIS

Force, and the threat of force, has always been a factor in the relationships between nations, but up to a generation ago its use could be to a certain extent limited to the areas under dispute.

Today, with the development of air power, rockets, and nuclear warheads, of chemical and germ warfare, the possibility of war imposes new responsibilities on world leaders. If they try to use only limited force they may find it inadequate, and move almost without realising it to a military involvement they had never bargained for, as the United States has done in Vietnam. If they use massive force in retaliation against an aggressor, they may find themselves, and the world, plunged into the horror of nuclear war.

The implications of this choice were probably never seen more clearly than by John F. Kennedy, President of the United States, and his brother Robert when, in the Cuba missile crisis of 1962, they faced the possibility of a war with Russia. It had been proved by reconaissance photographs that nuclear missile sites supplied by the Soviet Union were being built in Cuba, within striking distance of the United States.

Shadowed from the sea and air by the US Navy, a Soviet missile-carrying ship heads for Cuba.

President Kennedy resisted the arguments of his Joint Chiefs of Staff who favoured immediate military action. He decided first of all to try a less dangerous method—that of blockade. American ships were ordered to stop all Russian ships within 500 miles of Cuba, by force if necessary, to prevent further equipment reaching the Cuban missile sites. As reports came in of Russian merchant ships still steaming steadily ahead, bound for Cuba, the whole world waited tensely.

Then on the morning of 27 October a messenger brought in the news to the President that the ships had either stopped or already turned back to Russia. The risk of an American-Russian confrontation at sea was for the moment over—but reconaissance aircraft still reported that the work on the missile sites was proceeding rapidly. On 26 October had come a message to the President from Chairman Khrushchev which showed that he too was conscious of the horrors that a false step could unleash. He asserted that the weapons had only been sent to Cuba because he believed that the United States government was preparing to overthrow the Cuban government. 'If', he said, 'assurances were given that the President of the United States would not participate in an attack on Cuba, and would have the blockade lifted, then the question of the removal or destruction of the missile sites in Cuba would be an entirely different question.'

The restrained language of Khrushchev's letter gave at least the beginnings of hope, but the following day the situation was further confused by a second letter with totally different proposals. It made Russian removal of missiles from Cuba conditional on the removal of American missiles from Turkey. President Kennedy had already considered the withdrawal of the Jupiter missiles from Turkey—they were of doubtful strategic value. Nevertheless, if he concurred with Khrushchev's suggestion he might appear to be giving way before Soviet threats. The Joint Chiefs of Staff again urged an air strike against Cuba followed by an invasion.

Again the President hesitated—he realised so well what the implications might be. 'It isn't the first step that concerns me', he said, 'but both sides escalating to the fourth and fifth steps—and we don't go to the sixth because there is no one around to do so.' After many hours of discussion on the language and content of the letter to be sent as a reply to Khrushchev, the President's brother Robert Kennedy suggested that the first of the two letters—the more conciliatory one—should be sent, and that the United States should guarantee not to invade Cuba. The suggestion about the Turkish missiles was ignored. On 28 October another letter arrived from Chairman Khrushchev accepting the President's pledge, and agreeing to dismantle the missile sites. The President, his advisers, and the whole world, breathed more easily, and the threat of world war once more receded.

During the whole of the crisis, and the course of the debate within the American government as to what action should be taken, the President had been haunted, as Robert Kennedy tells us in his book *13 Days*, by the danger not only to his country but to the future of the world. 'He wanted to make sure that he had done everything in his power, everything conceivable to prevent such a catastrophe. Every opportunity was to be given to the Russians to find a peaceful settlement which would not diminish their national security or be a public humiliation. . . . The thought that disturbed him the most, and that made the prospect of war much more fearful than it would otherwise have been, was the spectre of the death of the children of this country and all the world—the young people . . . whose lives would be snuffed out like everyone else's.'

It was this realisation of the stakes involved—not only by Kennedy but by the Russian leader Nikita Khrushchev—that led to the eventual resolution of the crisis.

ESCALATION OF FORCE: VIETNAM

Before 1939 Indo-China—the area which now consists of Laos, Cambodia, and North and South Vietnam—was ruled by France. During the 1939–45 war the Japanese took over, and in Indo-China as in other Japanese controlled areas resistance groups soon formed, many of them dominated by communists. The active and growing communist party of Vietnam, led by Ho Chi Minh, formed the Vietminh (the League for the Independence of Vietnam) to work for the overthrow not only of Japanese but of French domination.

With the end of the war, and the defeat of Japan, the Vietminh quickly took over control of the whole of Vietnam, proclaimed its independence, and set up a government in Hanoi.

This proved to be only a temporary success. After the conference between the victorious powers at Potsdam, the French once more took over complete control of South Vietnam. They recognized Ho Chi Minh's state of North Vietnam only on condition that it became part of the French Indo-Chinese Federation, and that French troops were posted there.

These conditions were accepted by Ho Chi Minh, but the settlement did not last. The Vietminh asserted that the French were not keeping their side of the agreement, and on 19 December 1956 they launched an attack on the French troops in Hanoi. This was the first incident in a long and bitter war against French rule.

The French forces proved increasingly ineffectual against the Vietminh, stiffened as they were by a feeling for their country, and their belief in communism. It soon became clear that there was a real danger of a French defeat.

This possibility worried the United States government. President Eisenhower and his Secretary of State, John Foster Dulles, were determined to oppose the spread of communism anywhere in the world. They were convinced that if North Vietnam fell to the communists, then neighbouring countries would follow: South-east Asia would collapse 'like a pack of dominoes'. The American government was not prepared to see this happen, and decided to invest in a French victory—2.6 billion of military and economic aid for the authorities in Vietnam.

It was an investment that failed to pay off.

Despite American aid, the French were defeated at the siege of Dien Bien Phu in 1954, and all hopes of stalling a communist take-over by propping up French power were at an end. Many members of the United States administration were in favour of sending in American troops, but the President was discouraged by British disapproval and the opposition of the United States Army Command, who felt that such a step would not only be ineffective but also a positive danger to world peace.

At the Geneva conference, convened to seek a peaceful solution to the conflict, North Vietnam was handed over completely to the Vietminh. The United States refused to sign the agreement but guaranteed nevertheless not to work against it.

In 1956 the French left South Vietnam. This country too was now independent, under the Presidency of Ngo Dinh Diem, who tried to strengthen his authority by mounting an all-out attack on the communist elements in his country. His methods were ruthless; but so were those of Ho Chi Minh whose sweeping reorganization of land-tenure in the North is reckoned to have cost the lives of 50,000 peasants.

Diem's wholesale repression of any opposition made him more and more unpopular with all sections of the community, and on 20 December 1960, the National Liberation Front was formed to fight against him. It was theoretically a movement of many parties, but was in fact communist led, and became known to the anti-communists in South Vietnam as the Vietcong. By May 1961 the Vietcong's armed strength had increased from 3,000 to 12,000 men.

President Diem, alarmed by the growing communist threat, appealed to the United States government for further aid, and although John F. Kennedy, who was President, ruled out the idea of sending combat troops, he increased the number of American military advisers in South Vietnam from 800 to 17,000.

This proved inadequate in the face of the growing opposition to Diem's regime, and in November 1963 he was overthrown. A group of high-ranking army officers (a military junta) now took over power and the United States hoped for a breathing space in which their massive economic aid would help to stabilise the country.

Again their hopes were dashed. The North Vietnamese began to interfere directly in South Vietnam. By the end of 1964 the North Vietnamese authorities were helping to organise South Vietnamese guerilla fighters—men trained to fight in small groups, using unconventional methods.

In 1965 not only were the North Vietnamese helping with training, they were sending their own soldiers over the border to help the Vietcong in their struggle.

We have seen how up to this point each stage of the mounting communist campaign was countered by increasing or, as it is sometimes called, escalating, United States involvement. We now come to the most serious degree of escalation so far.

The United States was not only disturbed by North Vietnamese intervention; they were angered when three North Vietnamese torpedo boats in the Gulf of Tonkin fired on the US destroyer *Maddox*. On 4 August 1964, President Johnson, who had succeeded John Kennedy, interpreting the incident as 'open aggression on the high seas', ordered retaliatory air attacks on North Vietnam.

On 7 February 1965 there was further provocation. Vietcong guerillas attacked an American installation at Pluku, about 20 miles north of Saigon. Seven American soldiers were killed and 109 were wounded. President Johnson ordered the United States Air Force to attack barrack areas in North Vietnam, and on 28 February

The Vietnam War—Vietcong prisoners await interrogation.

announced a policy of continuous air strikes against the North. He believed that this policy would force the enemy into reaching a settlement.

But throughout 1965 the Vietcong showed no signs of wanting to give up the fight. Moreover there were signs that the South Vietnamese government in Saigon was in danger of collapse. President Johnson feared too the complete demoralization of the South Vietnamese army, infiltrated as it was by the communists, and frustrated by its lack of success against an elusive and fanatical enemy. He decided therefore on a further stage of escalation, to send, not just military advisers, but US fighting troops to Vietnam. By November there were 165,000 American combat soldiers in Vietnam; by the end of 1967 there were 500,000. The United States was now firmly committed to an extent undreamed of in the 1950s. America's anxiety not to give ground to the communists had led her into a war that became increasingly costly in both money and human life. The debate as to whether this policy was ever justified still goes on, and has seriously divided American opinion.

However the rights and wrongs of the Vietnamese intervention may finally be judged, it has already taught lessons to supporters and opponents alike.

It has demonstrated, even for a nation of enormous power like the United States, the difficulty of intervening effectively in the affairs of another country when the area of operations is thousands of miles away. In addition to the normal difficulties of communication and supply, and the problem of trying to understand the mind and strategy of an unconventional enemy, there has been the equally perplexing task of understanding the psychology of the people whom they are trying to help.

It has also brought home the bitter consequences of fighting guerillas hidden in villages belonging to the very people the forces were supposed to be defending. Many a commander had to face the dilemma of whether to destroy the homes of hundreds of innocent people in order to smoke out a handful of Vietcong. It has shown too the tremendous part that public opinion can now play in the prosecution of a war. It is extremely difficult for a government to play down its losses and defeats, or the effects of the war on the civilian population, if its own people are seeing the real evidence every day on their television screens.

Vietnam has seen the most powerful nation in the world decline to win a victory by using her nuclear power. The Americans could have ended the war at any time they chose by 'bombing Vietnam back into the Stone Age', a policy urged by a number of her politicians and service officials. It was a weapon that could have threatened our precarious world peace and the American government refused to use it.

RESPONSES TO VIOLENCE

Many men and women, sickened by the pain and misery that war and violence have imposed down the ages, have tried to eradicate it from their lives completely, and have refused to use it even for ends they believed to be right.

The Quakers (The Society of Friends) are a Christian sect founded by George Fox

Mahatma Gandhi, who tried to train his followers to use non-violent methods against the British.

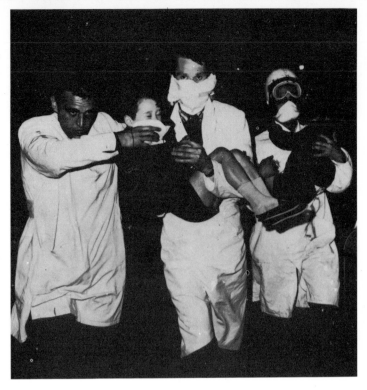

Violence is indiscriminate in its effects. These children are suffering from tear gas used in the Paris riots.

in the seventeenth century. They believe that violence and war are so foreign to Jesus's teaching that they are willing to be killed rather than save their lives by causing anyone else's death. Hundreds of Quakers during the world wars risked death serving in ambulance units, but they refused to do any job that would contribute to the fighting, and to the killing of other human beings.

Perhaps the most famous twentieth-century champion of non-violence was Mahatma Gandhi, the great Hindu leader, who inspired and organised the Indians in their struggle against British rule. He trained his followers to accept the doctrine of passive resistance. They defied the British authorities in every way they could, suffered imprisonment, went on hunger strike, but they refused to use violence in any form.

The doctrines of non-violence and pacifism are not to be dismissed as nonsense, still less as cowardice. They require a very high order of intelligent courage, and have often proved surprisingly effective. But there are very weighty objections to the pacifist idea. Many people feel that unless one arms oneself against aggression and is prepared to use force in return, countries and individuals can always be held to ransom, and that to defend one's cause, or one's family or country, one must be prepared in the last resort to fight.

Yet we have already seen the dangers of over-reacting to the threat of violence, in the Paris riots. There the use of force by the police, which in many cases was indiscriminate and uncontrolled, resulted in an escalation of violence, to a stiffening of the students' resistance and to considerable public revulsion. There have been similar instances at American universities, and in Chicago during the 1968 presidential

The United Nations General Assembly in session.

election. Police-action, as the London police proved in the Grosvenor Square incident of 17 March 1968, can be most effective and humane when carefully planned and supervised, and when the police follow the dictum of Winston Churchill when he was Home Secretary, that 'no more force should be used than is necessary to secure compliance with the law'.

In the face of tremendous international dangers, many people feel that our only hope of survival is to have a World Government, armed with sufficient power and force to insist on obedience. This alone they believe would compel the nations of the world to keep the peace. At the moment, our nearest approach to this is the United Nations Organisation—formed at the end of the Second World War not only to try and prevent war, but to help to organise a world in which war would have no point. It has not entirely succeeded.

It has no power to enforce obedience to its decisions and many small wars have broken out since its foundation. Yet it does provide a forum where representatives of more than a hundred nations can meet in public and in private to discuss their grievances. In times of world crisis the Secretary General of the United Nations has the great responsibility of seeking areas of agreement between the nations in conflict. The United Nations sends observers to ensure that a cease-fire between two countries is properly observed, as it did in 1967 after the Arab-Israel war. Sometimes it sends an international contingent of soldiers to impose order on a chaotic situation, as it did to the Congo in 1961.

Meanwhile, through the work of its agencies like FAO, WHO, UNESCO, and UNICEF, the United Nations wages its world-wide campaign to eliminate the poverty, injustice and ignorance that are so often at the roots of violence.

It is a human organisation and therefore an imperfect one, but with the support and help of its member countries it may yet ensure our survival.

FOLLOW-UP WORK

Make a collection of cuttings from newspapers which illustrate:
  (a) Man's determination to defend his territory.
  (b) An aggressive nation producing excuses for its aggression designed to lull world opinion.
  (c) Examples of student protest.

Do you think protesters are right or wrong to use violent means?

Study the non-violent methods used by Gandhi, Martin Luther King, by the Czechoslovakians after the Russian invasion of 1968. How far do you think their methods were effective?

Why did the countries who sympathised with Czechoslovakia not go to her aid?

Make a calendar of the events of the 13 days of the Cuba crisis.

Make a scrapbook illustrating the work of the United Nations.

FURTHER READING

Robert Kennedy, *Thirteen Days* (The Cuba Crisis).
Arthur Schlesinger, *The Bitter Heritage* (Vietnam).
Taya Zinkin, *Gandhi* (Methuen).
Nicholas Gillett, *Men against War* (Gollancz).
James L. Henderson, *Dag Hammarskjöld*.
Stephen King Hall, *Three Dictators* (Faber).
Joan Charnock, *Russia: The Land and Its People*.
Peter Wales, *World Affairs since 1919* (Methuen).
Wright Miller, *The U.S.S.R.* (Oxford University Press).
Malcolm Kruger, *Visual History of the United Nations* (Oak Tree Press).
Katharine Savage, *The Story of the United Nations* (Bodley Head).

6 MAN AND HIS ENVIRONMENT

There is a chance that in the next hundred years or so we shall make real progress in tackling the problems introduced to you in this book. Perhaps the world may at last become a more peaceful, more sensible place.

We shall still be left with the greatest problem of all. Will our earth still be the beautiful planet that the Apollo spacemen saw with such delight, or shall we have reduced it to a desolate waste? Will it still be able to support us, or shall we have squandered its riches by our carelessness and greed?

Man is a creature of this planet, made from earthly materials, kept alive by its atmosphere. For thousands of years he has settled in the areas which could most easily supply him with food and water. Sometimes he has been wasteful of the oppor-

An astronaut's view of Earth.

tunities offered him; sometimes, by intelligence and foresight he has preserved and even increased its riches.

For many centuries, whatever his achievements and his mistakes may have been, the effects of his labours—digging, quarrying, burning, wood chopping, hunting— were limited and localised. They made little difference to the earth or its atmosphere. But for us, living in the twentieth century, this is no longer so. There are now so many millions of us, all labouring to wrest a livelihood from our planet. We have discovered new sources of power—coal, oil, nuclear energy—and we are no longer midgets scrabbling harmlessly at the earth's surface. We can move mountains and rivers; we can work thousands of acres as one farm and mass produce goods by the million in our factories; we can fly beyond the speed of sound, send men to the moon. We are still at the mercy of earthquakes, volcanoes, storms and floods, but in many ways we can now wield a considerable power over our environment, and exploit it on a scale hitherto undreamed of.

How is this affecting our planet? What will be the consequences for us over the next hundred years? Many people fear disaster.

THE SOIL

Without soil the land would be dead—without vegetation, without animal life. Yet this soil is only a thin layer, never more than a few feet deep. It has taken millions of years to form, from the slow crumbling of the earth's crust, by the action of wind and water. Gradually, as the rock crumbled, it was invaded by microbes and by small primitive creatures like the earthworm, that penetrated it and fed on it, breaking it down to the fine consistency that allows seeds to germinate and grow. As plant life was established, binding the soil with its roots and shedding its dead leaves, the earth was further enriched. It has been a slow, complex, and delicate process, and man, by clumsy farming methods, has frequently upset it and lost the good crops that the soil could otherwise have given him.

The Greeks, for example, allowed their goats to graze unchecked on hillsides covered with woods and rich pastures; those hillsides are now brown and barren. In the same way flocks of Merino sheep grazed away for good much of the pasture land of Spain.

In the nineteenth and twentieth centuries the pioneer farmers of the United States pushed across their continent, intoxicated by the size and promise of their new lands, believing that in this part of the world at least the riches of nature could never be exhausted. They discarded the careful husbandry of New England, and grabbed what they wanted from the land. If they quickly exhausted its fertility they moved on—the frontier was still open. So they tore down forests and farmed rich prairies to the point of exhaustion. The ranchers of the West allowed their herds to range over the grasslands of the Great Plains, never withdrawing them to give the grass a chance to grow again.

By the end of the century the golden dream was over, the days of the moving

Sometimes man has been wasteful of the opportunities offered him—the Kansas dust bowl, 1939.

frontier were at an end. But millions more people were still moving in, not in small parties in covered waggons now, but hundreds at a time, travelling the railroads that now spanned the United States. The fertility of the land in many areas had already been reduced, and now with far more people to feed, the problem grew. Over thousands of acres the land was stripped of vegetation. The small particles of infertile soil were no longer bound together and began to be washed away by rain and blown by the wind.

By the 1930s farmers in Kansas, Oklahoma, Texas, and Colorado were suffering from this soil-erosion on a devastating scale. Their land, already poor because of intensive farming, was hit by drought year after year. In January 1933 a high wind struck Western Texas and the soil, by now reduced to dust, was blown away. Later in the same year more whirling winds in Kansas tore away thousands of acres of top soil. No part of the Great Plains escaped, and there was no respite—disaster struck year after year. Nine million acres were ruined, and so were many thousands of small farmers. In seven Colorado counties alone, a survey of 1936 showed that 2,811 farms out of 2,878 had been abandoned. Their owners were the victims not only of wind and drought, but of their own farming methods, which had reduced the once fertile soil to a barren dust.

Misguided attempts to improve land, without real understanding of the delicate balance on which its fertility depends, can also result in disaster.

Farmers in New Zealand, for instance, battling against useless scrub vegetation which kept invading their land, often used fire to hold it back. But the burnt land on the hillsides could no longer hold moisture and the water drained away, carrying with it tons of fertile soil.

Early European settlers in tropical Africa showed this same kind of well-meaning clumsiness. They viewed with a certain feeling of superiority the efforts of the African farmers who tilled only the surface of their soil, who grew crops apparently choked with weeds, and simply moved on to new clearings in the forest when the fertility of their original patch was exhausted. However, when European farmers introduced their own methods, they soon felt less confidence in their own abilities. Their ploughs certainly turned over the soil to a greater depth, but they went too far below the thin layer of top soil and mixed it with the infertile subsoil. They removed the weeds, but without them the soil was no longer bound together and was soon eroded by tropical rains. In the Savannah regions they introduced medicines to cure disease among the herds of animals, and the herds increased—but so did their capacity to

The results of erosion—Death Valley, California.

Sometimes by intelligence and foresight man has preserved and even increased Earth's riches. Careful terracing in Nepal.

eat grass, and in many areas the land was stripped of vegetation, and again it lay at the mercy of wind and rain.

Happily we can also find places in the world where man has shown understanding of the subtleties and complexities of the land he farms. For thousands of years there have been farmers who cared for their soil intelligently, practised simple rotation of crops, terraced their land along the contours of the mountains to prevent the water running off.

Nowadays we are trying not only to preserve the fertility already there, but to restore land that was once infertile and useless. It is vital that we do so in view of our increasing population, but it is a slow and expensive business, and it calls for great expertise to avoid the pitfalls of over-optimism and clumsy interference with nature that have so frequently led to disaster in the past.

We find one of the most dramatic examples of this land reclamation in Israel. Even before 1948 when Israel became a state, thousands of Jewish settlers were establishing their communities there, and beginning painfully to transform neglected and eroded land into fertile farmland. After 1948 the pace quickened as the Israelis began to build their country into a modern, productive nation. There was money coming in from Germany—as a reparation for Hitler's persecution of the Jews during the Nazi regime—and from the United States, in the form of gifts and aid. Israel was moreover highly endowed with trained and educated people, who were able to grasp and put into practice new techniques of farming based on a real understanding of soil-conservation. Farmers carefully ploughed along the contours of the hills to

reduce the surface run-off of rain. Lines of trees were planted to break the force of
the drying winds from the desert, and to bind the sandy soil together and prevent
it drifting. A pipeline was built to carry water from the Sea of Galilee to the Negev
desert, where the rainfall averages only an inch a year.

These are the kinds of projects that can restore and protect land ruined by abuse
or neglect, and they are beginning at last to transform many of the world's underdeveloped areas. Only in this way can we hope to hand on to future generations the
means to survive.

WATER

Human beings have occasionally survived for months without food. Without water
they cannot live for more than three days. From earliest times rivers and lakes have
provided us not only with drinking-water, but with the means to irrigate the land,
and also to carry away waste. For centuries water-power has been harnessed to
drive simple machines like mills, and more recently water has become vital to the
growth of industry, for it is an essential part of most industrial processes—it takes
20 tons of water to process a ton of steel—20,000 to produce enough paper for a
day's edition of a newspaper.

This pumping station in Israel is helping to bring fertility back to a once barren land.

The difficulty is to supply all the demands of factories and plants, to provide modern sewage systems for more and more people, and still to keep a plentiful supply of water pure enough to drink and healthy enough for fish to live in. The problem is greatest where large numbers of people are congregated. Even in Tudor times, London was finding it difficult to keep the 'sweet Thames' really sweet, because of the stubborn determination of Londoners to use it as a rubbish dump—a practice that went on unchecked for many centuries. The climax came in June 1858 when a hot summer and a low rainfall resulted in 'The Great Stink', when the river reeked from rotting refuse not only from houses, but from slaughter yards and sewers, and it was necessary to cover one's mouth and nose with a handkerchief before undertaking the smelly journey over Westminster Bridge!

By the twentieth century many cities were congratulating themselves on their fine new water services—sewage works designed to deal with urban waste before it reached the rivers, new enclosed drainage systems, and piped water to every home —and felt that their troubles were over. How wrong they were! As more and more factories were built, as populations increased, their supplies of clean water were again threatened.

Great new cities bring wealth and opportunity to the people who live there, but they also present tremendous and expensive problems of waste disposal to city councils and public health authorities, and make a colossal demand on water supplies. You can get some idea of the scale of the problem when you realise that in Inner London the authorities have to handle 187,000 million gallons of water-borne waste

River water polluted by detergents.

a year—over 25,000 gallons for each of the city's seven million inhabitants, who are catered for by the Metropolitan Water Board.

The millions of gallons of industrial effluent present a particular problem. Wherever factories and processing plants spew out waste into rivers and lakes, it all too often overpowers the bacteria which keep the water healthy. The rivers become filthy, smelly, and poisonous to fish.

The use of chemical fertilisers is essential if the world is to match its food supplies to its constantly increasing population. Yet the same fertilisers which are helping to feed us are also poisoning our water supplies. Millions of tons of nitrates and phosphates are washed by rain from the land into our rivers and lakes where they stimulate the growth of the plant life growing in the water. The water is choked with a dense proliferating weed, and soon becomes stagnant and dead. Lake Erie in Canada, once a fresh water lake of 9,000 square miles, has been turned by fertilisers draining from the surrounding land, and by factory waste, into a giant cess pool; to clean it up is going to cost $40 million.

The Rhine, once famous as one of the most beautiful of rivers, is now known as 'the open sewer of Europe' because of contamination of its waters by factory wastes. On 28 June 1969 the already polluted river produced a new danger point—shoals of dead fish were seen drifting down the Rhine, killed by an insecticide that had leaked into the river. Rotterdam, the Hague and Amsterdam, which use the Rhine as a water supply, had to turn to emergency supplies; the work of industrial plants was affected, and inland shipping was seriously disrupted.

Our power to wreck and spoil has now reached the point where we are threatening not just lakes and rivers, but even the seas around our coasts. After the Second World War, the volume of oil-tanker traffic on the seas increased considerably. These tankers, after discharging their cargo of oil, got rid of the thick sludgy residue at the bottom of their cargo compartments by pumping it into the sea. The patches of oil were all too frequently swept on to the nearest beaches.

In 1962, new methods of controlling tanker washings were introduced by the oil industry. 100,000 ton tankers can now clean out their compartments and yet only dribble out half a ton over a distance of miles. The effect on the beaches is negligible.

Unfortunately, however many precautions are taken, there is still the risk of an accident at sea. A notorious example was the *Torrey Canyon*. On 18 March 1967, this oil-tanker ran aground on the Seven Stones Rocks, 16 miles west of Lands End. She was carrying 119,000 tons of Kuwait crude oil. In the first few hours 30,000 tons of oil were lost, and when after vain attempts at salvage she broke up, another 50,000 tons followed. The danger from this oil to the holiday beaches of Cornwall was obvious, and the British Government gave the order to bomb the *Torrey Canyon* and so burn away as much as possible of the remaining oil.

Even so, large patches drifted to the coasts of England and France. Some of the first victims were birds—particularly the guillemots and puffins who dived into the glistening patches and were immobilised by the oil which clogged their feathers, or poisoned as they tried to preen it off.

Seabirds, killed by the oil that clung to their feathers, after the *Torrey Canyon* incident.

For many people living in the coastal towns, preparing to welcome the holiday visitors, the oil brought disaster. No one wants to sun-bathe on beaches contaminated with oil, and though expensive operations were mounted to spray the oil slicks and the beaches with detergent, and remove some of the thicker layers with machinery, thousands of holiday bookings were cancelled and the holiday trade was severely depressed.

AIR

'Her inhabitants breathe nothing but an impure and thick mist accompanied with a fuliginous and filthy vapour, which renders them obnoxious to a thousand inconveniences, corrupting the lungs and disordering the entire habit of their bodies, so that catarrh, coughs and consumption rage more in this one city than in the whole Earth besides.'

So wrote John Evelyn in the seventeenth century, showing that for Londoners, at

The *Torrey Canyon* aground on the Seven Stones rocks.

least, because of their novel practice of burning 'cole', air pollution was already a problem.

But for most people in those times it was unknown. They had a plentiful supply of pure air—air, that is, which contains 70 per cent nitrogen, 14 per cent oxygen, and ·003 per cent carbon dioxide. They did not know how lucky they were; they took it for granted.

But as more and more countries changed the basis of their economy from agriculture to industry, the 'hellish and dismal cloud belched out by thousands of chimneys' began to lie like a pall over industrial cities all over the world.

Whether they lived in Pittsburgh or Tokyo, Halifax or Frankfurt, people found that the smoke from the factories in which they worked, and from their own small fires, was ruining the quality of the air they breathed. New buildings so confidently built of the best quality stone, and so lavishly designed as the profits of industry mounted, were reduced to a uniform blackness. Washing put out to dry and babies put out for air could be covered with black smudges in a few minutes.

Far more serious: polluted air could be a killer. Breathed into the lungs, it irritated and inflamed the delicate mucous lining, and the incidence of lung disease, especially bronchitis, rose alarmingly in many industrial cities.

For many years nothing was done. The factory owners, the managers, and the professional classes merely moved out into new suburbs where they built homes far enough away—they hoped—to avoid the dirt. The workers themselves of course could not afford to move—they just had to endure it.

But industry did not stand still, it went on spreading, and it became impossible for anyone with concern for themselves, their workers or their city, to shrug off the problem. Gradually laws have been introduced to prevent the careless methods which had so largely contributed to the emission of soot and chemical fumes. Boilers and furnaces have been improved to get better combustion. In some cases ways have been found of trapping the smoke before it reaches the air. In certain areas, people are forbidden to burn ordinary coal in their fireplaces and obliged to use new types of smokeless fuel.

Gradually some cities, such as London, have begun to look less depressing. Buildings like St Paul's have been restored to their earlier magnificence with a fair certainty that for many years they will stay clean.

It is easy of course to *see* the connection between the smoke pouring out of chimneys and the pollution it produces. Other forms of air-pollution have not been so readily recognised or so easily dealt with.

California has always been famous for its warm sunny climate. This is why it became famous for fruit-growing, for film-making, and for its pleasure resorts. That climate was to prove a mixed blessing.

It was after the Second World War that people living in Los Angeles noticed a strange smell in the air, and an increased haziness. At first they thought it must be caused by fumes from the synthetic rubber plants that had been built during the war—but after the plants were closed, the acrid haze remained.

90

St. Louis blotted out by smog.

The main villain of the piece in this case turned out to be that most desirable status symbol of twentieth-century man, the automobile. Los Angeles is a wealthy place: the majority of families own at least one car, and the city boasts an astonishing system of urban motorways capable of handling dense flows of traffic.

But what was happening was that the exhaust of hundreds of thousands of cars was being irradiated by the much-prized sunshine of Los Angeles, producing a particular type of smog which was spoiling the atmosphere.

Any attempt to control this pollution had to give most prompt attention to the fumes from cars as well as from factories, and in 1960 a Motor Vehicle Pollution Control Board was established, whose work has proved of immense importance to other authorities all over the world.

Although Los Angeles, because of its particular locality and climate, is perhaps the most striking example, this problem of pollution, produced by the traffic and industry of a great modern city, is affecting people all over the United States. President Johnson summed it up when he signed the Air Quality Act of 1967. 'We are pouring at least 180 million tons of poison into the air each year . . . two-thirds of a ton for every man, woman and child in America. And tomorrow looks even blacker. By 1980 we will have a third more people in our cities . . . 40 per cent more automobiles and trucks. And the fuel we will be burning will be half as much again. Either we stop poisoning our air or we become a nation in gas masks, groping our way through dying cities and a wilderness of ghost towns.'

Students in Lund, Sweden, wear gas masks as part of their protest against the exhaust fumes from cars using streets in the city centre.

THE DANGERS OF PROGRESS

Our modern way of life has given us hitherto undreamed of opportunities, many of them for good. But it has also given us this terrifying power to wreck our surroundings. You can see this for yourself all around you—in your own home, and your own street.

Consider these random facts:

Each American citizen is throwing out 3/4 ton of solid refuse each year, and some of the new packaging materials are particularly difficult to destroy. And Europeans are not far behind in the amount of waste they produce.

Factory farming methods add to sewage disposal problems, because the excrement from the animals instead of being used as manure, is flushed away into the drains.

It is thought that because of the exhausts of jet planes, we are in danger of interfering with the thin ozone layer in the atmosphere which protects us from lethal ultra violet radiation from the sun.

Because of ruthless killing for profit, some of our animal species—the blue whale for instance—are in danger of being totally wiped out.

Thoughtless use of insecticides means the death not only of pests but of the birds that feed on them. Certain pesticides can have a harmful effect on man himself, if improperly used.

A constant watch must be kept by us the public, and the politicians who represent us, to see that these pitfalls are avoided. International control may be needed to see that dangerous insecticides are banned in all countries, not in just a few, and that cans of the lethal gas and viruses manufactured for germ warfare are not dumped irresponsibly into our seas.

92

The 1963 Test Ban Treaty confined the testing of all nuclear weapons to under-ground sites and so halted the frightening build-up of radiation in the atmosphere, but a continual guard has to be kept on nuclear plants used for peaceful purposes to see that they are completely under control.

We can no longer afford to blunder relentlessly on, grabbing what there is to grab and dumping our waste wherever it suits us. We have to remember that the earth's resources are not, in the light of present population figures and industrial demands, inexhaustible. We have to remember that our health and survival depend on our treating our planet with respect and care.

We must listen to the ecologists, the people who make a study of the delicate, inter-related ways in which the environment works. We must calculate carefully the effects of our actions, and realise that they are likely to upset all kinds of complex balances, that by being over-confident and over-ambitious in one area of the en-vironment we may create undreamed of problems in another.

We must face the fact that this is not going to be easy; it is certainly going to cost money. Factories may be induced to stop pumping waste into our rivers and air, but it will add considerably to their costs of production, and mean higher prices in the shops. Better and more efficient sewage schemes in our towns will mean higher rates. If the governments of the world begin, as they must, to assume more and more responsibility for tackling the problem, we shall have to pay higher taxes. We need to be prepared for this, and to realise we are paying for our survival.

Perhaps it would be as well if we learned from primitive man to think again of the earth as our mother, and to treat her not with the casual arrogance of spoiled children, but with the love and respect her generosity deserves.

FOLLOW-UP WORK ON CONSERVATION

Find out more examples of areas in the world whose physical appearance was changed by careless methods of farming.

Find out about the work being done to reclaim arid lands, e.g. the Sahara desert.

The problems of air and water pollution are being increasingly discussed in Europe and the United States. Make a collection of newspaper-cuttings of articles and public speeches which refer to these problems.

Find out what provisions are made for garbage disposal in your area.

Find out what laws have been passed in your country to prevent air pollution.

FURTHER READING

L. Dudley Stamp, *Our Developing World* (Faber).
Lorus and Margery Milne, *Water and Life* (Andre Deutsch).
Peter Scott, *Autobiography*.

FILMS

DISEASE

The Rival World, Unseen Enemies, Malaria, The Threat in the Water (Petroleum Films Bureau); *Victory over Pain* (Educational Films of Scotland); *Smoking and You* (C.O.I.); *The Fight Against Disease, The Story of Penicillin* (I.C.I.); *Dying for a Smoke or The Drag* (Concord Films Council).

HUNGER

Food or Famine (Petroleum Films Bureau); *The Land Must Provide* (Petroleum Films Bureau); *Borgo A Mozzano* (Petroleum Films Bureau); *The Rival World* (Petroleum Films Bureau); *The Desert Green* (Petroleum Films Bureau); *A Place of Happiness* (Petroleum Films Bureau).

LIVING IN AN INDUSTRIAL AGE

What About The Workers (2 parts) (Rank Film Library); *The Supervisors* (series) (B.B.C. T.V. Enterprises); *Planned Town* (Gaumont British); *The Lay Struggle* (B.B.C. T.V. Enterprises); *The Vanishing Coast* (Lewis Mumford, National Film Board of Canada); *Cast us not out* (Samaritan Films); *Death of a Factory* (Central Film Library); *People and Leisure* (Petroleum Films Bureau); *Dispute* (Central Film Library).

RACE

The Union of South Africa (Rank Film Library); *Ku Klux Klan* (B.B.C. T.V. Enterprises); *The First Americans* (B.B.C. T.V. Enterprises); *Bottom of the List* (World in Action—Granada T.V.); *February's Children* (World in Action—Granada T.V.); *No Entry* (World in Action—Granada T.V.).

VIOLENCE

World in Action—The Demonstration (Granada T.V. Film Library); *Stage for a Revolution, The Peacemakers* (Concord Films Council); *Stalingrad* (B.B.C. T.V. Enterprises).

MAN AND HIS ENVIRONMENT

Indus Waters (World Bank); *Water* (I.C.I.); *Shadow of Progress, The River Must Live* (Petroleum Films Bureau); *The Captive River* (Petroleum Films Bureau); *The Living Pattern* (Petroleum Films Bureau); *Look to the Land* (Petroleum Films Bureau); *Mekong* (Petroleum Films Bureau); *The World at Your Feet, Clean Air, Living Things are Everywhere, Clearing the Air* (National Film Board of Canada).

INDEX

The numbers in **heavy type** refer to the pages on which illustrations appear.

95